THE REAL
PATSY CLINE

THE REAL PATSY CLINE

Hoss! If you can't do it with feeling, don't. — Patsy Cline

THE REAL
PATSY CLINE

by Doug Hall

QUARRY
MUSIC
BOOKS

THE REAL PATSY CLINE

SW JH EA JB

The book *The Real Patsy Cline* is based on authorized interviews and research conducted for the film documentaries "The Real Patsy Cline" and "Remembering
Patsy," produced by Hallway Productions Inc. The quotation of lyrics from songs
performed by Patsy Cline is intended to illustrate the information and criticism
presented by the author and thus constitutes fair use under existing copyright con-
ventions. Every effort has been made to notify the publishers of these songs that
the lyrics have been quoted in this context. Photographs and documents illustrat-
ing the text are reproduced courtesy of Hallway Productions Inc., Country Music
Foundation, Sue Wilden, and Jimmy Walker. Thanks to Per Jonsson for creating
his Tribute To Patsy Cline world wide web site.

The publisher gratefully acknowledges the support of The Canada Council for
the Arts and the Department of Canadian Heritage for the arts of writing and
publishing in Canada.

ISBN 1-55082-213-6

Design by Susan Hannah.
Printed and bound in Canada by AGMV/Marquis, Cap-St.-Ignace, Quebec.
Published by Quarry Press Inc., P.O. Box 1061, Kingston, Ontario K7L 4Y5
Canada, www. quarrypress.com

CONTENTS

For my granddaughters

Nicole, Katelyn
Abigail, Stephanie

Patsy Cline had the voice of an angel, a career fraught with triumph and disaster, and a private life that exceeded any scriptwriter's imagination. In a blazing career of less than eight years, she recorded over 100 songs (51 singles for 4 Star Records and 51 for Decca Records) and four albums — PATSY CLINE, SHOWCASE (WITH THE JORDANAIRES), SENTIMENTALLY YOURS, and THE PATSY CLINE STORY, recorded the month before her death. Many of Patsy's recordings, including *Walkin' After Midnight, I Fall To Pieces, Crazy, She's Got You, Faded Love*, and *Sweet Dreams*, charted high on both country and pop charts, making her one of the first successful "crossover" artists. These songs have become evergreen classics. During her career, she received numerous *Billboard, Cashbox, Music Vendor*, and *Music Reporter* awards such as the Favorite Female Artist and Star of the Year, winning 10 such awards in 1962, the most ever won by a female country artist in one year. Patsy Cline was inducted into the Country Music Hall of Fame in 1973, the first solo woman artist to be so honored, and into the Recording Hall of Fame at the Grammy Awards in 1992 for her recording of Willie Nelson's *Crazy*. In 1995 Patsy Cline was honored at the Grammy Awards for Lifetime Achievement in Music. Then in 1997 the American Music Operator's Association (AMOA) presented plaques to Charlie Dick, Patsy's husband, and their daughter Julie (Dick) Fudge on TNN's *Prime Time Country* honoring *Crazy* as the Number 1 Juke Box single of all time and *I Fall To Pieces* as Number 17 out of the all-time top 20.

Surprisingly, Patsy never had a million-selling record during her short career; the gold and platinum records came after her death. More than 30 years later her music is still topping the charts, though. As of 1 October 1998, the platinum album PATSY CLINE'S GREATEST HITS, first released in 1967, had been on *Billboard's* Top Country Catalog Album Chart for an astounding 601 continuous weeks. During that period it was Number 1 for 251 weeks. The album is constantly selling and her records are being played on America's juke boxes. BMG has featured 20 of her songs on THE ESSENTIAL PATSY CLINE, joining such country legends as Eddy Arnold, Chet Atkins, Willie Nelson, Jim Reeves, and

Skeeter Davis in this prestigious "Essential Series" of albums. The definitive PATSY CLINE COLLECTION, a four CD boxed set of 104 recordings, was compiled by the Country Music Foundation for release in 1991.

A further indication of her enduring popularity are the touring companies of the musicals *Always . . . Patsy Cline* and *A Closer Walk with Patsy Cline* which chart her rise from honky-tonk road-house singer to Grand Ole Opry, Carnegie Hall, and Las Vegas star. These reviews have played to sold-out audiences off-Broadway, at Nashville's Ryman Auditorium, in Las Vegas and in theaters across the United States and Canada. After portraying Patsy as Loretta Lynn's close friend in the critically and commercially successful movie *The Coal Miner's Daughter* in 1980, Hollywood devoted a dramatic film to Patsy's career in *Sweet Dreams* in 1985, with the soundtrack going platinum. The extent of her following can also be seen on the world wide web, where several sites are devoted to Patsy Cline and her fans, most notably "A Tribute to Patsy Cline" (www.nola.ovik.se/pj/patsy), maintained in Sweden by Per Jonsson and dedicated to keeping the memory of Patsy Cline alive, while in her home town of Winchester, Virginia, hundreds of fans gather each September 8th on her birthday to celebrate Patsy's life, visiting such landmarks as her family homes on South Kent Street, her grave in Shenandoah Memorial Park, Gaunt's Drugstore, and the Kurtz Cultural Center, where the collection of Patsy Cline memorabilia includes the fur stole she wore to the Country Music Festival awards ceremonies in 1962. The Always Patsy Cline Fan Club is also based in Winchester. A stamp has been issued to commemorate her achievement — there is even a special breed of hybrid tea rose named in her honor, the cultivar "Patsy Cline." Year by year Patsy Cline's fame only grows, never fades.

Patsy's voice was a rare instrument. Many country and pop singers have tried to copy her style but have never equalled her ability in interpreting a lyric or caressing a melody. The legendary Nashville producer, Owen Bradley, who died on 7 January 1998, was the catalyst for much of Patsy's recording success. He was a superb arranger with an uncanny knack for choosing the right songs. He also knew how to soothe, prod, enrage, and stroke the mercurial Patsy, at just the right moment. He forced her to rise to the melodic heights he knew she was capable of reaching. Patsy was able to tear at the heartstrings with singles such as *She's Got You* and then do a complete turnabout with the bluesy *Walkin' After Midnight*, which composer Don Hecht called "pure B-flat blues."

Patsy Cline is the bench-mark by which any female artist, who has ever covered a country song, is measured, from Loretta Lynn and Tammy Wynette to Reba McEntire and k.d. lang, Trisha Yearwood, and LeAnn Rimes. Loretta Lynn still honors her courage in making room for women country artists in a chauvinist world. "Patsy was my idol as well as my friend. She opened the door for all the girls singers, including me." As Trisha Yearwood adds, "She definitely broke some rules. Somebody had to do it, and she was the one."

PC

This book is based on authorized interviews and research conducted for the production of two complementary film documentaries on her life and career, *Remembering Patsy* and *The Real Patsy Cline*, which have been telecast, on commercial and cable television, in the United States, Canada, and the United Kingdom in addition to more than fifteen other countries in three languages. Both productions are available in platinum-selling home videos, *The Real Patsy Cline* from White Star and *Remembering Patsy Cline* from ABC Video in their prestigious "Legends of Country Music" series.

Much of the information gathered from interviews with forty-eight of Patsy's friends and family, totalling over sixty hours, could not be included in these one-hour documentaries, however. The wealth of candid interviews concerning Patsy's early years in Winchester, Virginia, recording sessions in Nashville, appearances on Jimmy Dean's *Town and Country Times* and *Arthur Godfrey's Talent Scouts*, her extensive tours of America, Hawaii, and Canada, her ground-breaking debuts on the stage at Carnegie Hall, in Las Vegas, and at the Hollywood Bowl, her tragic death in a plane crash near Camden, Tennessee, and her revolutionary and enduring impact upon the music industry had to be culled and refined. Because a one-hour television "special" is only forty-seven minutes, thirty-seconds long in order to accommodate commercial time, only some of the insightful comments about this icon of country music had to be selected. The book *The Real Patsy Cline* includes not only the substance of the two documentaries but also much of what had to be left out due to these restraints.

We already know a great deal about the facts of Patsy's life from existing biographies, which, unfortunately, have taken considerable license with these facts while extrapolating them into melodrama. This book adds new shadings to her personal and professional image which others have often colored in with conjecture and titillation. Those who knew her best were more than willing to talk about her, including Becky Green Miller, Patsy's childhood friend, Elsie Mae and Hunter Gaunt, who gave her a job in their drugstore. WINC Radio disk jockey Phil Whitney who thought Patsy was a diamond in the rough, and fellow disk jockey, Jim McCoy, who was persuaded by Patsy to let her perform on radio for the first time. Songwriter Hank Cochran who co-wrote one of her biggest hits, *I Fall To Pieces*, which his wife Jan Howard assumed she would be recording. The late Owen Bradley, Patsy's legendary producer, tells stories about the highs and lows of her recording sessions and her choice of songs. George Hamilton IV and Jimmy Dean recall a tour of western Canada riding and drinking with Patsy in the back seat of a Cadillac during a snowstorm. Loretta Lynn brings to life that magic moment when she was first summoned by Patsy to her hospital bedside after Loretta dedicated her rendition of *I Fall To Pieces*, performed on Ernest Tubbs' *Midnight Jamboree*, to Patsy who was recovering from a near-fatal automobile accident. Willie Nelson tells the story of *Crazy*, the song he wrote and Patsy performed, which launched his Nashville career as a songwriter. Dottie West, Patsy's best friend in the music business, takes us behind the scenes at her final concert in Kansas City, an interview captured before Dottie's own untimely death in an automobile accident. And her Canadian friend and confidant Anne Armstrong opens up her collection of letters received from Patsy, letters that let us hear Patsy talking in her own voice about everything from her kid's laundry and choice of wardrobe to her conquest of Carnegie Hall and Las Vegas. The late rockabilly legend Carl Perkins takes us on a pilgrimage to the site of the fatal plane crash in Tennessee to find some record of Patsy's life. Patsy's daughter Julie Fudge and her husband Charlie Dick let us get to know her domestic charm and extravagances. k.d. lang explains why she and her backing band "The Re-Clines" approached Patsy's producer Owen Bradley to produce her Patsy-Cline-sound-alike album SHADOWLAND. These are some members of the cast who recreate for us the romance and the comedy, the tragedy and the irony of her life and times — who tell the story of the *real* Patsy Cline.

Anne Armstrong:
Anne Armstrong was one of Patsy's true confidants. During their friendship, which began when Anne met Patsy at a performance in Hamilton, Ontario, Canada, Patsy kept in touch by letter and revealed a side that few of her fans ever knew, perhaps because Anne was a "safe" correspondent in a foreign country.

Bill Anderson:
A country singer best known as "Whispering Bill" and for his frequent appearances on the Grand Ole Opry, Bill Anderson achieved success as a songwriter with a number of hits, including *City Lights*, *Once A Day*, and *Saginaw, Michigan*.

Eddy Arnold:
When Patsy hit Nashville and began her climb to country music stardom, Eddy Arnold had become the first country music superstar, who, nevertheless, was overwhelmed by Patsy's talent.

Margie Beaver:
Patsy, like most entertainers, did not have a host of close friends because of the pressures of a recording and touring career. True friends like Margie Beaver were valued.

"Big Daddy" Blair:
Patsy loved and trusted her Nashville neighbor Henry Blair and gave him the pet name "Big Daddy." She sought his advise on personal matters.

Joyce Blair:
Joyce Blair, affectionately called "Blair" by Patsy, and "Big Daddy" were godparents to Patsy and Charlie's children. "Blair" was faithful to Patsy's last request to care for her children should she ever die.

Owen Bradley:
There are two Nashville producers who have become legendary — Chet Atkins and Owen Bradley. Bradley was the musical genius who produced Patsy's greatest hits. When k.d. lang reprised Patsy's sound, she approached Bradley to produce her album SHADOWLAND.

CAST

Harold Bradley: Patsy was backed by some of the finest session players in Nashville, including guitar players like Owen Bradley's brother, Harold.

Bill Braese: The manager of the Dyersburg Airport, Bill Braese warned Randy Hughes, Patsy's manager and the pilot of her fatal flight, about the danger of trying to reach Nashville in a storm on 5 March 1963.

Evelyn Braese: Evelyn Braese was the co-manager of the Dyersburg Airport who spoke to Patsy just before the last leg of her flight and life.

Roy Clark: Country recording artist and television star of *Hee Haw* Roy Clark, a fellow performer on Jimmy Dean's *Town & Country Time*, remembers Patsy as much for her generosity of spirit as for her singing talent as he witnessed her rise to fame.

Hank Cochran: Patsy's interpretation of Hank Cochran's songs like *I Fall To Pieces* and *She's Got You* made them immortal and made a place for him in country music history.

Charlie Dick: Patsy married the ebullient Charlie Dick on 15 September 1957. Ever since Patsy's untimely death, Charlie has kept her memory and music alive through his extraordinary promotional skills while administering the Patsy Cline Estate.

Roy Drusky: Country star Roy Drusky turned down Owen Bradley's offer to record *I Fall To Pieces* because he thought it was a girl's song. His instincts were confirmed when the song became one of the first women's country music anthems in the hands of Patsy Cline.

Julie (Dick) Fudge: Patsy's first child offers special insight into her mother's life and career, even though she was only four years old when her mother died.

Elsie Mae Gaunt: Patsy worked behind the soda fountain of Gaunts' Drug Store in Winchester, Virginia. Elsie Mae Gaunt encouraged her to audition to appear on *Arthur Godfrey's Talent Scouts*, the most influential entertainment program on television in the late 1950s.

Hunter Gaunt: Patsy caused drug store owner Hunter Gaunt no end of problems by booking off to perform at dances and in honky tonks around Winchester; he often filled in for her to keep the peace with the other girls working at the store.

Jim Glaser: A member of The Glaser Brothers who backed up Patsy at the Mint Casino in Las Vegas, Jim Glaser vividly recalls the creation of this unique show, one of the first performances by a female country artist in Vegas.

George Hamilton IV: Patsy enjoyed embarrassing the country singer George Hamilton IV, who performed with Patsy on *Town & Country Time* and received his big break, like Patsy, on *Arthur Godfrey's Talent Scouts*.

Don Helms: It has been said that only a valet truly knows the character of his master; session players like steel guitarist Don Helms saw Patsy in the raw light of the recording studio.

Harlan Howard: Harlan Howard co-wrote *I Fall To Pieces* with Hank Cochran as well as the country classics *Pick Me Up On My Way Down* and *Heartaches By The Number*.

Jan Howard: Jan Howard fell in love with *I Fall To Pieces* the moment she heard it and recorded the first demo, but her husband turned the song over to Patsy. While she lost the song to Patsy, Jan made a new friend.

Ferlin Husky: Ferlin Husky shared the same management company and performed with Patsy on television and on the road, including Pearl Harbor, Hawaii, and was charmed by her presence, on stage and off.

Mavis Husky: Young Mavis Husky first came under Patsy's spell when she was sixteen but did not meet her idol until she came to Nashville. Patsy would leave a lasting impression on the next generation of women country singers like Mavis.

George Jones: Country music's "Living Legend" George Jones worked many shows with Patsy, including the Hollywood Bowl and her final appearance in Kansas City. His influence on the sound of country music singing has been no less remarkable than Patsy's.

k.d. lang: Many people have compared k.d. lang's voice to Patsy's; some have even gone as far as to suggest that she is the reincarnation of Patsy, an impression k.d. herself sometimes felt.

Neil Leroy: Neil Leroy worked at Dyersburg Airport, providing pilots with weather briefings. Although he advised Randy Hughes, pilot of the plane which crashed with Patsy on board, not to fly into the storm, Hughes did not heed the warning.

Ken Leggitt: Ken Leggitt, a licensed pilot, drove to the crash site with the Police Chief of Paris, Tennessee, and provides an eyewitness report.

Loretta Lynn: Loretta Lynn dedicated her version of *I Fall To Pieces* to Patsy who was in the hospital following a near fatal car accident. Patsy heard this "angel" singing her song and asked Charlie to track her down. A firm friendship was established.

Neil Matthews Jr.: A member of The Jordanaires, Neil Matthews Jr. sang backup for many artists but none as talented and charismatic as Patsy. "We'll never forget having a chance to work with Patsy Cline."

Becky Green Miller: Becky Green Miller knew Patsy in Winchester when she was known as "Ginny" Hensley and witnessed her life and career from local amateur hour performances through her marriages to Gerald Cline and then Charlie Dick.

Jim McCoy: Jim McCoy was a disk jockey at WINC Radio, Winchester, and vividly recalls the day Patsy came to the station and said she wanted to sing on radio. "Everybody knew that this gal could sing."

Willie Nelson: When Patsy recorded his song *Crazy*, Willie Nelson was known as "Hugh." He was a struggling songwriter who had recently arrived in Nashville.

Harry "Hap" Peebles: Country music deejay and promoter Hap Peebles promoted the final Patsy Cline performance in Kansas City.

Carl Perkins: Upon hearing about her fatal plane crash, rockabilly star Carl Perkins traveled to the site along with other performers like Roger Miller and collected some of her personal belongings, now on display at the Country Music Hall of Fame. For Perkins, Patsy was the epitome of country music when she recorded his song *So Wrong*.

George Riddle: George Riddle sang on the Hollywood Bowl show with Patsy and marveled at her charismatic stage presence.

Sylvia: Country singer Sylvia was only six when Patsy was killed but no other artist has so influenced her singing style. When she first heard her sing *Crazy* time stood still.

Lisa Stewart: Like Sylvia, Lisa Stewart pays homage to Patsy's memory and influence, recognizing that Patsy's style of singing shaped the sound of the next two generations of female country singers.

Marsha Thornton: Long before she became a country singer, a friend played one of Patsy's records for Marsha Thornton when she was eight years old. From that moment on she was a fan.

Mel Tillis: Mel Tillis, in addition to being a country singing star and a class act, is an accomplished songwriter who wrote *Strange*, which Patsy recorded on 25 August 1960, another hit for her, and toured with Patsy and Brenda Lee.

Billy Walker: Renowned country artist Billy Walker asked Patsy to perform in Kansas City at a benefit concert for the late Cactus Jack Call. If fate hadn't intervened, Patsy's last show would have been Billy's last show, too, but he chose not to fly back with Patsy to Nashville, giving up his seat to Hawkshaw Hawkins.

Ray Walker: Ray Walker, another Jordanaire, backed Patsy on her major recordings for Decca and on stage at the Grand Ole Opry, where he recalls his last conversation with her.

Dottie West: Like Patsy, Dottie West's life and career as a country singing star was cut short by a tragic accident on 4 September 1991, but during Patsy's years in Nashville they became the closest of friends and confidants.

Phil Whitney: The General Manager of WINC Radio in Winchester, Virginia, Phil Whitney helped to launch Patsy's career.

Del Wood: Country singer and honky tonk pianist Del Wood appreciated Patsy as the first "cross-over" artist who was at once a country and a pop music star.

Trisha Yearwood: As one of country music's most popular woman singers, Trisha Yearwood knows that the emotional power of Patsy's music makes her as appealing today as yesterday. "You believe every word."

1932: Patsy is born Virginia Patterson Hensley, September 8, Winchester, Virginia, the daughter of Sam and Hilda Hensley.

1936: Patsy wins top honors in a tap dancing competition, in imitation of her childhood idol, Shirley Temple.

1940: Patsy learns how to play piano by ear at age eight.

1944: Patsy works at age twelve in a Rockingham, Virginia, poultry factory plucking chickens, to help support her family.

1945: Patsy suffers from rheumatic fever with serious throat infection which deepens her voice.

1947: Patsy's parents separate and she lives with her mother in Winchester, Virginia.

1948: Patsy quits school to work at Gaunt's drugstore in Winchester.

1948: Patsy auditions for Phil Whitney, General Manager of WINC Radio, and becomes a member of Joltin' Jim McCoy's broadcasts.

1948: Patsy is invited by Wally Fowler to audition, unsuccessfully, for WSM Radio, the home of the Grand Ole Opry, in Nashville, Tennessee.

1951: Patsy becomes a regular performer at the Rainbow Inn in Winchester, Virginia.

1952: Patsy fronts Bill Peer and the Melody Boys on the honky tonk circuit; Peer dubs her "Patsy" after her middle name, Patterson.

1953: Patsy marries construction business heir Gerald Cline, March 7.

1953: Patsy is introduced as his discovery of the week by Ernest Tubb on his show *Midnight Jamboree*, broadcast on WSM Radio each Saturday after the Grand Old Opry.

CHRONOLOGY

1954: Patsy wins the fourth annual National Championship Country Music Contest in Warrenton, Virginia, and becomes a member of *Town & Country Times*, hosted by influential booking agent Connie B. Gay and starring Jimmy Dean and His Texas Wildcats, with regular appearances by Roy Clark and George Hamilton IV, broadcast on WARL, Arlington.

1954: Patsy records *It Wasn't God Who Made Honky Tonk Angels* by Kitty Wells, then the reigning woman country music artist.

1954: Patsy signs a recording contract with the California-based 4 Star Records on September 30.

1955: Patsy records her first Extended Play (EP) 45, SONGS BY PATSY CLINE, on June 20, including *A Church, A Courtroom And Then Goodbye, Honky Tonk Merry-Go-Round, Turn the Cards Slowly*, and *Hidin' Out*.

1955: Patsy first appears on the Grand Ole Opry during the Ralston-Purina show, hosted by Ernest Tubb.

1956: Patsy records *Walkin' After Midnight* with Owen Bradley as producer on November 8 for 4 Star, which becomes a Number 3 hit after her performance on *Arthur Godfrey's Talent Scouts*.

1957: Patsy wins the talent competition with her performance of *Walkin' After Midnight* on *Arthur Godfrey's Talent Scouts* on January 21.

1957: Patsy records her first LP album on Decca, PATSY CLINE, released on August 5.

1957: Patsy's divorce from Gerald Cline is finalized. Later that year, she marries Charlie Dick.

1958: Patsy gives birth to daughter Julie Simadore Dick on August 25.

1960: Patsy becomes an official member of the Grand Ole Opry, fulfilling a childhood dream.

1960: Patsy records *I Fall To Pieces* on November 16, soon to become her first Number 1 country music hit.

1961: Patsy gives birth to son Allen Randolph "Randy" on February 8.

1961: Patsy is nearly killed in a car accident on June 14, and Loretta Lynn sings *I Fall To Pieces* for her benefit on Ernest Tubb's *Midnight Jamboree*.

1961: While recovering from her accident, Patsy makes a triumphant return to the Grand Ole Opry stage in a wheelchair.

1961: Patsy records songs for her second album, SHOWCASE (WITH THE JORDANAIRES) in August, including *Crazy*, which is released as a single on October 16 and rises to the top of the *Billboard* country charts and into the top ten on the pop charts.

1961: Patsy appears on the first all-country bill at Carnegie Hall with Jim Reeves, Minnie Pearl, Grandpa Jones, Bill Munroe, and Faron Young on November 29.

1961: Patsy records her next Number 1 hit, *She's Got You*, on December 17.

1962: Patsy records her third album, SENTIMENTALLY YOURS, released June 8.

1962: Patsy performs with Johnny Cash, George Jones, and other country singers at the Hollywood Bowl in June.

1962: Patsy receives 10 awards at the Country Music Festival awards ceremonies in Nashville, setting a precedent and displacing Kitty Wells as the most highly honored female country artist.

1962: Patsy performs at the Mint Casino Lounge in Las Vegas for five weeks over Christmas.

1963: Patsy records several songs, including *Faded Love* and *Sweet Dreams*, during a week-long session in February with Owen Bradley. The songs would be included in her last album, THE PATSY CLINE STORY, released after her death.

1963: Patsy agrees to perform for free with Hawkshaw Hawkins, Dottie West, Billy Walker, George Jones, Cowboy Copas, and others for the "Cactus" Jack Call benefit concert in Kansas City on March 2.

1963: Patsy, Randy Hughes, Hawkshaw Hawkins, and Cowboy Copas die when their plane crashes on March 5 near Camden, Tennessee.

1973: Patsy is elected to the Country Music Hall of Fame.

1985: The Hollywood film interpretation of Patsy's life, *Sweet Dreams*, is released by Tri-Star.

1986: The Hallway Productions authorized video biography, *The Real Patsy Cline*, is released for international distribution as a television special and home video, to "set the record straight," in Charlie Dick's words.

1990: The musicals *Always . . . Patsy* and *A Closer Walk with Patsy Cline* begin touring North America.

1991: *The Patsy Cline Collection*, produced by the Country Music Foundation and compiled by Paul Kingsbury, is released by MCA Records, the first complete chronological survey of her recording career.

1991: Hallway Productions releases a second authorized video biography of Patsy Cline, *Remembering Patsy*, featuring information, interviews, images, and film footage of Patsy performing not previously available.

BILLBOARD CHARTED SINGLES

Country	Pop	Song Title
2	12	Walkin' After Midnight
14	–	A Poor Man's Roses
1	12	I Fall To Pieces
2	9	Crazy
–	99	Who Can I Count On
1	14	She's Got You
–	97	Strange
10	53	When I Get Through With You
21	90	Imagine That
14	85	So Wrong
–	73	Heartaches
8	83	Leavin' On Your Mind
5	44	Sweet Dreams
7	96	Faded Love
47	–	When You Need A Laugh
23	–	He Called Me Baby

Patsy performing live on WINC, Winchester, Virginia, her home town.

August 26, 1961

Dear Pearl:

Thank you so much for wanting to start my own fan club. Here's the background story on me, Patsy Cline.

I was born September 8, 1932. I started playing piano when I was eight years old and played by ear. Can't read notes and don't know what key I sing in. At fourteen I started singing on the Saturday Country Music Show on WINC Radio and that led to playing in clubs around Winchester. I worked in the drug store during the day and sang at night.

A tv promoter and producer named Connie B. Gay heard me on the radio and took me to Jimmy Dean in Washington, DC. That was a big step and got me on tv with guest spots on national tv.

I got a contract with 4 Star Records. "A Church, A Courtroom And Then Goodbye" was my first single with the Coral label. I did three auditions for the Arthur Godfrey Talent Scouts show. Then on January 21, 1957 I won the contest and stayed with the show for two weeks. I sang "Walkin' After Midnight," which was released on Decca Records. It made Number 2 on the charts. . . .

Always,
Patsy Cline

When Patsy Cline wrote this autobiographical letter to the founder of her first fan club in 1961, she was on the verge of becoming the most famous female country artist of all time, with the recording of country and pop crossover classics *Walkin' After Midnight* and *I Fall To Pieces* behind her and the recording of *Crazy*, *She's Got You*, *Faded Love*, and *Sweet Dreams* before her. Ten years after her tragic death in 1963, Patsy Cline was inducted into the Country Music Hall of Fame, the first solo woman artist to be so highly honored. Her path to the Country Music Hall of Fame led from the hamlet of Gore in the far northwest corner of Virginia near the West Virginia border, where she first lived after being born, through the town of Winchester where she grew up, to Jimmy Dean's *Town and Country Time* jamboree in Washington, DC, where she caught the attention of talent scout Arthur Godfrey — then south about 700 miles to Nashville and the Grand Ole Opry and beyond to Las Vegas, Hollywood, Hawaii. But when she was growing up in northern Virginia that 700 mile road down through the Shenandoah Valley to Music City might as well have been 7,000 miles long.

For a child born during the Depression in small-town America, Patsy Cline's childhood was not all that unusual, except for her drive to become a performing artist. She was born Virginia Patterson Hensley on 8 September 1932 to Sam Hensley, a blacksmith and mechanic by trade, and Hilda Hensley, a seamstress of note, who had married in 1927 when Sam was forty years old and Hilda fifteen. For the first twelve years of her life Patsy lived a somewhat nomadic life with her parents as they moved from Gore to Elkton to Grottoes to Portsmouth, Virginia, while her father found work as a quarryman, fireman, blacksmith, and engineer during these lean years. Along the way, Patsy's brother, Samuel "Sam" Lawrence, and sister, Sylvia Mae, were born, and Patsy contributed to the family's welfare by working at a poultry factory in Rockingham, plucking chickens when she was twelve years old. The family finally settled, at least geographically, in Winchester when Patsy was in Grade 8, moving into a small house on South Kent Street in a working-class district close to downtown, but her parents were at odds and separated when she was fifteen.

Patsy's childhood idol was the legendary Shirley Temple, and somehow she taught herself the rudiments of dance, winning an amateur tap-dancing contest in Lexington, Virginia, when she was only four years old. When she was seven, her parents purchased a piano for her after repeated pleas to do so, and Patsy soon learned to play by ear, inspired by her half-sister, an accomplished pianist. Her other musical inspiration was the radio broadcasts of the Grand Ole Opry on WSM, Nashville. Even before she was ten, Patsy became an avid listener of the Opry and would sing along with Roy Acuff, Eddy Arnold, Kitty Wells, and the other Opry regulars.

Her own singing 'career' began in the Baptist Church choir in Winchester where she also sang solo and in duet with her mother. When she was thirteen Patsy suffered a seriously infected throat, a complication of rheumatic fever, as she told a reporter in 1957 while explaining the distinctive quality of her voice. "I had a serious bout with rheumatic fever when I was thirteen. I developed a terrible throat infection and my heart even stopped beating. The doctor put me in an oxygen tent. You might say it was my return to the living after several days that launched me as a singer. The fever affected my throat and when I recovered I had this booming voice like Kate Smith's."

One of Patsy's childhood friends from Winchester who took her seriously when she said she wanted to become a country music singer was Becky Green Miller. "We used to call her Ginny," Becky remembers. "She sang even then and she was good. We had a little local amateur hour and she did quite a few of those shows. We didn't have pyjama parties in those days. Mothers were too busy for that kind of thing. We worked after school and didn't have a lot of time for socializing."

Patsy worked hard to contribute to her separated mother's household. She was sixteen years old when she quit school and walked into Gaunt's Drug Store in downtown Winchester looking for a job. Upon first meeting, Hunter Gaunt liked her. "The first time I met Patsy was when she arrived at my drug store. She said she needed a job and needed one bad. I told her that the only job open was behind the soda fountain and I'd think it over and let her know. She came back the next morning and was so insistent about needing a job that I hired her — she went to work that afternoon."

Hunter Gaunt's wife, Elsie Mae, didn't have a grown grand-daughter and soon took Patsy under her wing, encouraging her to pursue her music career, suggesting she try to audition for *Arthur Godfrey's Talent Scouts* program. "We really liked her," Elsie fondly recalls, "but it was obvious she needed more education. She was curious about everything and asked questions. I tried to answer them to the best of my ability. She loved music and was always singing. It was at that time she began singing in public at places like the Orchard Inn. My husband and I weren't the instigators but we did suggest that she should try to get on *Arthur Godfrey's Talent Scouts*, which she eventually did."

With her employers' encouragement, Patsy began to perform at local inns, clubs, and bars in the Winchester area. Hunter Gaunt remained patient with Patsy even as her music career began to disrupt the day-to-day operation of his drugstore. The more in demand Patsy became, the more problems it caused at Gaunt's Drug Store. The other girls initially co-operated with Patsy and switched night duties with her when she was performing but they soon started to balk. "When she asked for time off we'd give it. But it did create problems with the other girls because it was usually when we needed her and schedules had to be juggled.

"I'll never forget one night when she desperately wanted to go to Frederick for a benefit. As far as I can remember, Jimmy Dean was in the group she wanted to sing with. 'Mr. Gaunt, I have a commitment and I'm desperate. So and so won't change with me.' It was a Saturday night. The soda fountain wasn't too busy on Saturday nights, so I told her to go ahead and I covered for her."

While she was working at Gaunt's drugstore, Patsy pursued her musical aspirations, relentlessly, not only traveling around the region to perform at inns and clubs, but also begging Phil Whitney, General Manager of the local radio station WINC for an audition. "I met Patsy in the late '40s," Whitney remembers. "We weren't country then, we were hillbilly. I remember Patsy coming to the studio. It had a big picture window in the waiting

HUNTER GAUNT

ELSIE MAE GAUNT

PHIL WHITNEY

room and the control room was right off it. I can remember her walking right up to the window. She pushed her nose right up to the glass and looked in. One day she said she wanted to sing. There was an announcer by the name of John Morgan. He said let her sing. We heard her sing and everybody knew that this gal could sing."

At the time, Jim McCoy was a disk jockey at WINC Radio, but unlike Phil Whitney, he wasn't impressed when he first met Patsy. "When Patsy came to WINC, back in the late '40s, she was a diamond in the rough. Frankly, at the beginning, she wasn't all that great — it took a few years. She had a big heart and wanted one thing more than anything else and that was to be a success and show the people of Winchester that she could do it."

Patsy also pressed her will to become a country singer on gospel singing legend Wally Fowler whose show was broadcast from the Ryman Auditorium on WSM following the Grand Ole Opry. When Fowler and his Oak Ridge Quartet played Winchester's Palace Theater, Patsy audaciously approached him for an audition. At first sceptical, Fowler was overwhelmed when her heard Patsy's voice and gave her a spot on his show that evening. He also invited her to come to Nashville and try out for the Opry. Opry chief John Denny auditioned her, with Moon Mullican accompanying Patsy on piano, but she received a 'don't call us we'll call you' response. Nevertheless, Roy Acuff overheard the audition and asked her to sing on his *Noon-Time Neighbors* show on WSM, confirming her faith in her own talents and steeling her resolve to return to Nashville one day and perform on the Opry stage.

Back in Winchester, Patsy continue to perform on WINC and to play the honky tonk circuit in the early 1950s, appearing regularly at such roadhouse haunts as the Rainbow Inn dressed in what would become her trademark cowgirl outfits sewn by her seamstress mother. At the Moose Lodge in Brunswick, Maryland, Patsy eventually hooked up with Bill Peer and his Melody Boys. Peer took on the role of managing Patsy's career, convincing her to change her name from Virginia

Hensley to 'Patsy' Hensley, based on her given middle name, Patterson. During this period, she also met Gerald Cline, who gave her a new family name when they married on 7 March 1953.

With the help of Bill Peer, Patsy was invited back to the Grand Ole Opry by Peer's acquaintance, Ernest Tubb, the Texas Troubadour, in April 1953, and while she did not perform on the Opry show itself, she was introduced as the discovery of the week by Tubb on his *Midnight Jamboree* show which followed the Opry on WSM, broadcast from the Ernest Tubb Record Shop around the corner from the Ryman Auditorium. Patsy's next step on the road to becoming a professional country singer came when she won the fourth annual National Championship Country Music Contest, sponsored by WMAL Washington broadcaster and booking agent Connie B. Gay, who awarded her $100 as Best Female Vocalist, a weekday job singing commercials on WMAL, and a regular spot on the afternoon show *Town & Country Time*, broadcast on Gay's sister station WARL Arlington, starring Jimmy Dean and his Texas Wildcats. Gay also produced Patsy's first recording during this time, a cover of *It Wasn't God Who Made Honky Tonk Angels*, which reigning "Country Queen" Kitty Wells had taken to Number 1 on the charts in 1952.

Jimmy Dean and other "Town & Country" regulars like Roy Clark and George Hamilton IV all remember Patsy's stunning stage presence, clear talent, and spunk. Roy Clark recalls the first time he saw Patsy perform. "I can see it like it was yesterday. She had on a black dress, high heels, with a flower in her hair, or was it on her dress. She looked like a country girl come to town. She turned to the band and said, 'Well y'all know *Walkin' the Dog*, a Webb Pierce song.' I said yes, so we kicked it off. Patsy just took over and instead of the band backing Patsy Cline up Patsy Cline led the band wherever she wanted them to go. Absolutely tore the roof off. People in the audience stopped their conversations, they stopped drinking and literally jumped up on their feet and screamed. She had to have confidence in her voice because when she sang a song, that song had been sung."

During 1953, Bill Peer began circulating demonstration recordings of Patsy's singing to various record companies, and during a talent scouting trip to Washington, William A. McCall, president of the California-based independent label 4 Star Records who had signed

ROY CLARK

Jimmy Dean earlier, offered Patsy her first recording contract. Patsy was just three weeks past her twenty-second birthday when she signed the agreement with 4 Star on 30 September 1954. Bill Peer witnessed the three page, sixteen paragraph, contract.

Despite her enthusiasm at signing a recording contract, there is no way the terms could be construed as being even remotely fair to Patsy, especially when they are compared to the contracts that Columbia Records were offering to artists such as Marty Robbins, Ray Price, or Carl Smith at the time. Columbia's royalty rate was 5 per cent; Patsy signed for 2.34 percent, less than half. It was a day when singles sold for 75 or 85 cents retail. When dealer discounts and returns were factored in, the profit margin was small, to say the least. In those days a bestselling country single was 25,000 units, which would thus gross $20,000 or less. At 5 per cent royalty, the artist would realize $1,000; in Patsy's case, even if she were to have a smash hit, she would have been most fortunate to realize $500. In addition, the fees 4 Star paid to session musicians at American Federation of Music scale would be deducted from her royalties when earned.

Setting aside the meager royalty and these charge backs or recoupables, the most disturbing thing about the contract was Clause 3: "Recordings will be made at recording sessions, in our studios, at mutually agreeable times during the term hereof. A minimum of 16 r.p.m. record sides, or the equivalent thereof, shall be recorded during the period of this contract, and additional recordings shall be made at our election. The musical compositions to be recorded shall be mutually agreed upon between you and us, and each recording shall be subject to our approval as satisfactory, for manufacture and sale." In effect, Patsy could only record songs published by 4 Star Music, the song publishing arm of the record label, or songs approved by 4 Star.

In late November 1954, Patsy headed to New York with Bill Peer and the band to record a demo session for Paul Cohen, who was in charge of country A&R (artist and repertoire) for Decca Records and who was considering 'leasing' Patsy Cline from 4 Star. Cohen had previously shepherded Red Foley, Webb Pierce, and Kitty Wells into the Decca fold. They recorded demos of two 4 Star songs — *Turn the Cards Slowly* and *Three Cigarettes (In An Ashtray)* — and two others approved by 4 Star — *Crazy Arms* and *This Ole House*. Peer also arranged for Patsy to audition for *Arthur Godfrey's Talent Scouts*, perhaps the most important television variety show at the time. While the producers of the show were keen to have Patsy perform, they wanted her to appear solo, without Bill Peer and the Melody Boys. Patsy refused to perform without her band.

Paul Cohen was sufficiently impressed by Patsy's demo sessions that he tried to purchase her contract from Bill McCall at 4 Star, but McCall would agree only to lease Patsy's recordings to Decca for distribution. Cohen nevertheless managed to gain control of the recording sessions and arranged for Patsy to record her first four singles at a Nashville studio on 1 June 1955 — *A Church, A Courtroom And Then Goodbye, Hidin' Out, Turn The Cards Slowly, Honky Tonk Merry-Go-Round*. Her first single on the 4 Star Coral label was *A Church, A Courtroom And Then Goodbye*, released 20 July 1955. While the lyrics of *Honky Tonk Merry-Go-Round* recalled her years of working the honky-tonk circuit, *A Church, A Courtroom And Then Goodbye* took on personal meaning as her marriage to Gerald Cline began to collapse, eventually resulting in their divorce in 1957.

Honky Tonk Merry-Go-Round

I'm a honky tonk merry-go-round,
Making every spot in town;
Starting out early, coming home late,
Every night I'm with a brand new date.

I'm a honky tonk merry-go-round,
Acting like a foolish clown;
Still racing those blues that they leave with me,
A wondering if I'll ever be free.

'Round and 'round I go,
Riding high and feeling low;
'Round and 'round just like a top,
Well, I'm a-getting dizzy but I can't stop ...

(Lyrics by Frank Simon and Stan Gardner, copyright 1955
by 4 Star Music Company, renewed by Acuff-Rose Music, Inc.)

A Church, A Courtroom And Then Goodbye

The first scene was the church,
Then the altar
Where we claimed each other . . .
My next scene was a crowded courtroom,
And strangers we sat side by side.
Then I heard the judge make his decision,
And no longer were we man and wife . . .

(Lyrics by Eddie Miller and W.S. Stevenson, copyright 1955
by 4 Star Music Company, renewed by Acuff-Rose Music, Inc.)

Patsy entered the recording studio again on 5 January 1956 to record her first Extended Play 45, featuring the 4 Star songs *I Love You Honey*, *Come On In (And Make Yourself At Home)*, *I Cried All The Way To The Altar*, and *I Don't Wanta*. None of these songs charted, nor did the four songs she recorded 22 April 1956, *Stop, Look And Listen*, *I've Loved And Lost Again*, *Dear God*, and *He Will Do For You*.

Patsy's label-mate at 4 Star Records and fellow "Town & Country" performer Roy Clark remembers those early days recording with Patsy and Jimmy Dean. "4 Star Records was the other extension of radio and television. There was a recording studio there — if you want to call it that. It was a room that had a recording machine in it. This was back in the days where the next step, if you were playing clubs, was to hear yourself on radio. It wasn't about having big hit records, that was a distant dream. It was a co-op thing. Jimmy Dean would go on one day and record and we'd all back him up. The next day I'd go in and they would back me up and the same with Patsy."

To overcome these problems, Paul Cohen of Decca had hired Owen Bradley to produce Patsy's songs, a man who would prove to be the creator of the Patsy Cline "sound." Bradley had been told that making Patsy into a recording star would be a challenge; however, he discovered a kindred spirit. "I had met Patsy a few years before when Decca Records made arrangements to lease her from 4 Star and asked me if I would record her," Bradley recalls. "I was told she was not too easy to get along with and a few weeks later she came to see me along with her then husband, Gerald Cline. I found her very pleasant. She

**ROY
CLARK**

was just like me — she was trying to get along. It was an early assign-ment for me as an A&R (artist and repertory) man. I was trying to get started in the line and she was trying to become a singer. We were sort of in the same boat.

"4 Star would send many songs to Patsy and they would send a copy to me. I have no idea about any of the actual details except that we would not be allowed to record any songs except those songs. *Walkin' After Midnight* was a 4 Star song and a good one. It became her first hit record.

"I remember one time she came to Nashville, and I said, 'Patsy, I just don't see how we can record, we don't have any songs that are really that good.' She cried a little bit and said, 'I don't have much money or anything. I really need to record so I can get some money.' I suggested that maybe we could do a couple of hymns. We recorded *A Closer Walk With Thee* and *Life's Railway To Heaven*. Later I was surprised to learn that the very last song Patsy ever sang professionally was *Life's Railway To Heaven*. She was on the 'Cactus' Jack Call ben-efit show in Kansas City, Kansas — it was Sunday, March 3, 1963."

OWEN
BRADLEY

Following the recording of her first EP in June 1955, Patsy dis-tributed in person advance copies to the music establishment and appeared at Nashville's Centennial Park on 26 June 1955 in concert with headliner Ernest Tubb and his Texas Troubadours. According to *Billboard* magazine, over 15,000 fans were in the audience when new recording artist "Patsy Kline" performed. A week later on July 2, Patsy fulfilled her childhood dream when she appeared on the Grand Ole Opry during the Ralston-Purina sponsored section of the show, host-ed by her old champion and now dear friend, Ernest Tubb. Patsy Cline was now a bona fide professional country singer but she would not become a star until she recorded *Walkin' After Midnight* on 8 November 1956 and performed it on *Arthur Godfrey's Talent Scouts*, 21 January 1957.

Despite becoming a new star in the Music City galaxy, Patsy remained a small-town girl throughout her career, often returning to the Winchester area to visit friends and family — and to sing at the local American Legion, for example, or again on her home radio sta-tion, WINC, though not always receiving a home-town-hero recep-tion, as general manager Phil Whitney recalls. "The men all liked

Patsy but some of the women didn't. She would call and say to book her for a show. She would want to come back home. She'd pick up a few dollars and see momma. The last one I remember working with her was the Winchester Drive-In and the Drive-In over at Harper's Ferry. I think it was a jealous streak because when the guys would start clapping the women started booing. I remember Patsy just breaking down and crying. Why are the people of Winchester treating me like this? She was a good looking gal. She had made it by then, and I think the people in Winchester couldn't accept that she had made it."

PHIL WHITNEY

Still, old friends, like Elsie Mae Gaunt, saw Patsy in another light. She never forgot her days at the drug store and the kindness of the Gaunts. When she appeared at Winchester's Apple Blossom Festival in 1956 and returned to be the Grand Marshal of the parade in 1959, Patsy made it a point to visit them. "She was there in all her glory but she was the same person we knew. I never saw her in a bad mood. She stopped by for a visit at our house on Washington Street."

Come On In (And Make Yourself At Home), the song she recorded during her second session in the Decca studio, seemed to be written just for her and the home-town folk of Winchester, Virginia.

Come On In (And Make Yourself At Home)

Come on in
And sit right down.
And make yourself at home.
If I had one wish, I wish I could
Go back to my old neighborhood,
Where the good folks, they all love you as their own....
I'd sing their praises long and loud
'Cause they're all my folks and I'm mighty proud
Of the little old town
Back home where I was born.

ELSIE MAE GAUNT

(by V.F. Stewart, copyright 1955, 4 Star Music Company, renewed by Acuff-Rose Music, Inc.)

Over the course of her career Patsy's style of delivery would often be called "down-home," though her first hit record was the decidedly "up-town" *Walkin' After Midnight*.

Patsy backstage during her honky-tonk years.

Patsy's first home in Gore, Virginia.

Patsy's home on South Kent Street in Winchester, Virginia.

Gaunt's Drugstore, where Patsy worked at the soda fountain.

Patsy in her mid-teen years when she signed herself "Virginia."

Patsy performing with the Kountry Krackers (top) and photographed with George Hamilton IV (left) and Jimmy Dean (above) on Town and Country Time, *circa 1956.*

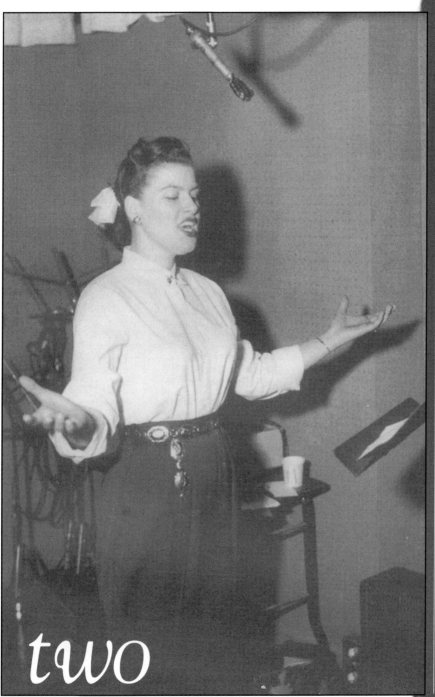

two

Patsy recording at Owen Bradley's studio in Nashville, circa 1957.

PATSY CLINE

Patsy Cline waited two rather long years to appear on the Arthur Godfrey "Talent Scout" television program. When the time came, she sang a song called "Walkin' After Midnight," and the result was overwhelming. Her Decca recording of the song became a top hit, and Patsy Cline became a singing sensation almost instantly. Obviously, she won the Godfrey contest and has been winning the hearts of countless enthusiastic fans throughout the country ever since.

This is Patsy's first Decca album. It is an album that had to be made. It is the answer to a truly staggering popular demand. The reaction to her records has been unusually immediate and enthusiastic. In this album, Patsy Cline displays her wonderful talent for singing "pops" — and does a bang-up job on a group of new, delightful tunes . . .

After appearing on the Wally Fowler show, Patsy made personal appearances on such TV shows as "Grand Ole Opry", and appeared with stars like Ernest Tubb and other leading country artists. It wasn't until the "Talent Scout" appearance, however, that her career really started to climb at a meteoric clip. Her fabulously successful recording of "Walkin' After Midnight" has been followed by other great hits like "Today, Tomorrow And Forever," coupled with "Try Again" and "Stop, Look And Listen," coupled with "I've Loved And Lost Again."

Here is an album-sized treat — jam-packed with the delightful voice and captivating personality that made Patsy Cline the newest darling of the vocal world. Listen as Patsy Cline sings her wonderful way through dozens of tuneful melodies . . . and right into your heart.

— from the liner notes of Patsy's first album in 1957.

During the blush of her initial success as a recording artist and Nashville performer, Patsy fell in love with Charlie Dick, whom she married on 15 September 1957. Charlie picks up the story of their romance and Patsy's growing fame. The first time Charlie saw Patsy she was in an old-time black minstrel show he attended. "It was at Handley High School," Charlie recalls. "As far as I remember she did a song and dance number — a gay nineties. She wasn't Patsy then; she was Virginia Hensley. I had no idea who she was because I'd never heard that name in town. I found out she was working at Gaunt's. Later on in the year she told me that she had to quit school and went to work. She had a couple of jobs before the drug store — at a meat packing plant and at a bus terminal as a waitress.

"A few years later I did hear that a local girl had gotten a recording contract, which was big news for our town. The next time I heard Patsy sing was on the way back home from a National Guard Camp where I was stationed. I was riding with another guy and we heard a record on the radio. It was Patsy, and I remember saying 'good singer.'

CHARLIE DICK

"I was running around with some of the boys from Winchester and one had a brother-in-law who played in a country band, the Kountry Krackers. They played a lot of dance halls, armories, American Legions, skating rinks, beer joints in and around Winchester, and I started to go to the Berryville National Guard Armory to hear them. Patsy was on the Jimmy Dean show, out of Washington, at the time, but she'd sing with the Crackers on Friday night and do the Jimmy Dean show on Saturday night.

"One night I went up and asked her to dance and she said she couldn't dance while she was working — so I walked off. Later I see her dancing with somebody, so I went back and asked her to dance again.

"She said, 'No, I can't dance while I'm working!'

"'Why hell, I just seen ya dancing with somebody.'

"'Well, that's my husband.'

"A couple of weeks later I saw she didn't have her husband around, so I went back and asked her to dance, and she finally did dance with me. We got along pretty good, and the following week I invited her out to my friends car for a drink — there wasn't any drinking allowed in the dance hall.

"I asked her out and she said she had to go to Washington to do the Jimmy Dean show and suggested that I take her. I said great! But, I had a problem. I didn't have a car. Mine was wrecked, so I conned my friend, Howard Snap, into driving us to Washington.

By that time Patsy and Gerald had separated and she had moved back home to live with her mother Hilda Patterson Hensley."

BECKY
GREEN
MILLER

Becky Green Miller was also witness to the affection Charlie and Patsy shared for one another. "Charlie was the kind of happy-go-lucky guy that all the girls liked, not just Patsy. She really wanted Charlie and she was going to have Charlie Dick or else. Nothing, or nobody, or anything was going to stand in her way. When she started going with Charlie, I followed her ups and downs, her joys and tragedies. That's what I remember about Patsy, but I think most of all I really knew how much she loved Charlie."

Charlie's mother, Mary, had a difficult time believing that her son was dating Patsy Cline, a bona-fide country music singer in her mind, as Charlie recalls. "I told my mother that I was going to a Marine base. She asked who with? I told her Patsy Cline. She'd seen her on TV. Hell, somebody on TV don't usually fool around with characters like me. I still don't think she believed I was going with Patsy until she pulled up in front of the house and picked me up. Once we got back, Patsy and my mother got along real well. I

CHARLIE
DICK

didn't realize how well 'till later on. They used to sit and talk after I went to work in the morning and they talked pretty good. They got along fine. Great!"

Arthur Godfrey Talent Scouts was one of the number one entertainment program on television at the time — the only thing bigger was Godfrey's monumental ego — where many singing careers were launched, including Patsy's. The format was simple. The performer would be introduced by someone playing talent scout. The only condition was that the talent scout could not be a relative. The performers competed with each other for prizes. First prize was a week-long booking on Godfrey's morning radio show. As Charlie explains, Patsy knew that a successful performance on *Talent Scouts* would advance her career into the national spotlight. He accompanied her to her second audition, this time without Bill Peers and the Melody Boys. "The second audition, which she set up herself, came pretty soon after we met. I went with her to New York. For the audition it was Patsy in the studio with an older lady on the piano and myself. An engineer and some other guy were in the control room. Patsy was more nervous than I ever saw her in my life. Don't ask me why, she just was. She didn't sing good at all.

"They said, 'don't call us, we'll call you.' So we left. We just figured they didn't want us and it's gone. Forget it."

Patsy and Charlie returned to Winchester and she continued to perform on *Town and Country Time*, now broadcast on Saturday night television as *Town and Country Jamboree*, commonly known as the "Jimmy Dean Show." For Patsy, it was more than unsettling to find out that a fellow performer on the show, nineteen-year-old George Hamilton IV, had been successful with Godfrey's producers. Hamilton was riding the crest of his 1956 hit *A Rose And A Baby Ruth*, which would become a million-seller once boosted by his appearances on Godfrey's shows.

Patsy's sense of injustice at the hands of Arthur Godfrey soon disappeared when she received another invitation to audition, as Charlie Dick remembers. "One Saturday night, a few weeks later, things began to happen. I think it was Dale Turner who came running into the dressing room and said for everybody to do their best. Godfrey would be watching at his home in Leesburg, Virginia, about thirty-five miles out of Washington. The following week Patsy got a call from the Godfrey show asking her if she could come to New York. Naturally she said, 'Sure!'

"Patsy took off for New York with her cowgirl clothes, her mother, Hilda, and a friend who agreed to act as talent scout. First off, the Godfrey people didn't like the cowgirl clothes, and Patsy didn't get to sing one of her songs that she really liked. She ran through all her favorite songs. They didn't like any of them until she got to *Walkin' After Midnight*, which she had recorded on

November 8, 1956. Even though it was to become one of her greatest hits, she didn't like it. She said it didn't make much sense wandering around after midnight looking for someone."

Walkin' After Midnight

I go out walkin' after midnight,
Out in the moonlight,
Just like we used to do.
I'm always walkin' after midnight,
Searching for you.
I'll walk for miles along the highway,
That's just my way of being close to you.
I go out walkin' after midnight,
Searchin' for you.
I stop to see a weepin' willow
Cryin' on his pillow.
Maybe he's cryin' for me.
And as the sky turns gloomy,
Night winds whisper to me.
I'm lonely, as lonely as can be.

Off-camera, Godfrey wasn't one to take lightly or fool with. He didn't appreciate deception, but in this instance he had a sense of humor, as Charlie explains. "For some reason Hilda's friend got cold feet and wouldn't play talent scout, so Hilda went on using her name. Evidently, someone told Godfrey about it later, but he just laughed and said it wouldn't have made a difference."

"Godfrey was so impressed with Patsy that she did two weeks on his radio show instead of one, and she was called back a number of other times. Godfrey even booked her on his top-rated Wednesday night television show *Arthur Godfrey and His Friends*. I'm pretty sure that Pat Boone and the McGuire Sisters were on that show with her.

"Patsy's record company was off on the word 'mark' and capitalized on the exposure she and *Walkin' After Midnight* were getting," Charlie Dick states. "The song shot up the pop and country charts. Appearing on Godfrey's shows was the biggest career break she ever had." *Walkin' After Midnight* was recorded during Patsy's fourth recording session, along with *The Heart You Break May Be Your Own, Pick Me Up On Your Way Down*, and *A Poor Man's Roses*, which appeared on the B side. *Walkin' After Midnight* would peak at Number 2 on the *Billboard* country music chart and, remarkably, at Number 12 on the pop chart, one of the first "crossover" hits by a female country singer.

Patsy's "Town and Country" colleague and soon-to-be national touring colleague George Hamilton IV also remembers her performances on the Jimmy Dean and Godfrey shows — and the national success of *Walkin' After Midnight*. As a nineteen-year-old singer from Winston Salem, North Carolina, George first met Patsy when he was booked on *Town and Country Times*. "It was the biggest thing I'd ever appeared on. It was regional network that covered several cities in the Northeast. One of the featured stars was Patsy Cline. Boy! I was impressed when I saw and heard her. She was wearing a cowgirl outfit with rhinestones. I remember the thing that struck me was her powerful personality. She had charisma, stage presence, confidence — all the things I lacked. I was scared to death. Here was this gal that came on like gang busters. When she hit that stage it was her stage, it was her audience."

GEORGE
HAMILTON
IV

George would be the first to say that Patsy's appearance on *Talent Scouts* and Godfrey's endorsement made his performance pale by comparison. "Boy! She just blew them away. Mr. Godfrey fell in love with her. She really set the woods on fire. Once she won and became such a favorite of Mr. Godfrey's, everybody was talking about her. She became a national name and *Walkin' After Midnight* became a national hit. It was a pop hit, not just a country hit.

"She was quite different from Kitty Wells and a lot of girl country singers. She was a crossover. She was accepted in the pop field."

As Charlie Dick suggests, Patsy's "crossover" appeal was created, in part, by the orchestration the Godfrey show musicians provided, a sound that may have influenced Owen Bradley when producing subsequent recordings. "Her appearances probably had a lot to do with her producer, Owen Bradley, making her music a little more 'uptown' instead of the pure country sound she had before. When you worked with Godfrey, you worked with a full orchestra. Even though you did country songs, you were performing with a twenty-piece orchestra. I don't know if Owen Bradley got the idea from that, or if he already had the idea or not, but I think her appearances were instrumental in her changing route a little bit."

CHARLIE
DICK

The Godfrey show appearances did indeed raise Patsy's national profile, and soon she was touring the continent by car, bus, train and plane, routes she would trace again and again until her death. Before the Godfrey show, Patsy had performed primarily in Maryland, Washington D.C, West Virginia, and Virginia, with the occasional trip to Nashville to appear on the Grand Ole Opry and with Red Foley (Pat Boone's father-in-law) on his *Ozark Jubilee* show, broadcast on ABC-TV from Springfield, Missouri. Now she was being booked out of Nashville on thirty-day tours, traveling back to New York to appear on *The Alan Freed Show* and afar to perform on shows like Tex Ritter's *Western Ranch Party* in Los Angeles, joining Porter Wagoner and thirteen-year-old sensation Brenda Lee on one tour, Mel Tillis and Brenda on another, even venturing into Canada with other country performers, like her old "Town and Country" friends, Jimmy Dean and George Hamilton IV. Mel Tillis, who would co-write Patsy's 1962 hit *So Wrong* with Carl Perkins and Danny Dill, remembers Patsy's spirit in those early days touring the country by car. "We went out on tour with Brenda Lee. Brenda was only eleven years old. I drove Brenda's mother, Grace, Patsy and Brenda Lee all over. Patsy was a real trooper. Yeah! I loved her."

MEL
TILLIS

As George Hamilton recalls, such rigorous tour schedules made for strange behavior. "I was on tour, in western Canada with Jimmy Dean and Patsy. And, of course, we were doing a lot of reminiscing about the old days in Washington. We were in a Cadillac and I was in the back seat between Patsy and Jimmy. They were passing a bottle back and forth and taking a few nips and I was trying to sleep 'cause it was early in the morning and we were driving through a snow storm. Patsy and Jimmy got happier, and happier, and then they got to crying and talking about the good ol' days. Suddenly they got mad, 'cause they realized I wasn't drinking with them.

"Patsy turned to me and asked, 'Hey Hoss, who do you think you are?'

"I asked, 'What do you mean?'

"Patsy snapped back, 'You sitting there high and mighty like you are some kind of a saint and we're having us a good time remembering the good ol' days, and you ain't even had a drink with us.'

"So I joined in and soon we were passing the bottle back and forth. Needless to say, by the time we got to the town where we were supposed to do a Sunday afternoon show the three of us were in rare form indeed. I don't remember what kind of show we did but it must have been unusual.

"I played a lot of shows dates with Patsy. Those were great days. It was a lot of fun but I think we underestimated her. We all worked with her and we took for granted that she sang really good — she sang great! She had all this charisma and stage presence but she was a good ol' gal from Winchester and she was easy to be friendly and folksy with, just one of the guys. She didn't have pomp and circumstance.

"When you sit back and listen to her records, they were away ahead of their time. She sounds as good today as anything being recorded."

Hamilton touches on the apparently dichotomy in Patsy's character: her reputation for being tough was legendary but so was her gentle concern for others. "She could cuss and was not hesitant to lay one on you. But she was never cold, never mean or petty. If you were cocky, or arrogant, she could pull you off your high horse in about three seconds. She was strong but she was a lady, and underneath there was a gentle caring person. Patsy had a gift from God and used it with authority, with confidence and taste — she was an artist."

When Roy Clark was a young man looking for a break in

GEORGE HAMILTON IV

the music business while working as a session player for 4 Star Records on Patsy recordings, he was on the receiving end of Patsy's generosity. There would be very few in the country music business who would have done what she did. "Bill McCall was the owner of 4 Star Records. I'll never forget one time we were at the recording studio and I'm backing. McCall sent a letter to the studio saying, 'Have *Roy Clark* record this tune and don't say anything to Jimmy Dean.' Unbeknown to me he sent another letter saying, 'Have *Jimmy Dean* record this tune and don't say anything to Roy Clark.' You always thought you were the most important one.

"One night I'm working at The Famous bar and the phone rings. The waitress comes up and says, Patsy Cline's on the phone for you. Patsy said, 'You recorded a song and I was wondering did you record it to release it?' I was blown away that Patsy knew that I had recorded that song. She hadn't been around when I did it and I'd only done it a week before.

"I said, 'Yes and as far as I know they plan to release it as a single.'

"Patsy said, 'Well they sent me your record to learn and they want me to record it.' Well, it broke my heart. I mean all of a sudden I wasn't that important. It really crushed me. I still have that feeling when I think about it.

"I'm sitting there, in this pay phone booth, and I finally get my wits about me. I said, 'Well Patsy, I guess that's the way it is. Go ahead and record it. It won't bother me if that's the way they want to do it.'

"Patsy says, 'No Hoss! If they want to get somebody to record it, they'll get somebody else because I don't play that way.' That was the moment that I found out all there was to Patsy Cline."

Patsy didn't like people who came on with the "big-to-do" and had no problem letting them know it, as Charlie Dick notes. "People would come up and ask her for autographs. She didn't mind signing autographs because she asked for them herself. When we were in Vegas she asked Della Reese for one. If Della had stuck her head up and walked off, she might have heard something as she walked away. There was a couple of people at the Opry that I

ROY
CLARK

CHARLIE
DICK

think she thought had a big head and she would say to me, I hope to hell I never get like that."

Patsy was in Nashville staying at June Carter's house when Charlie came home one day and found greetings from the President of the United States. "Uncle Sam wanted my body at Fort Bragg, North Carolina," Charlie recalls. "I had to report — you know, I think it was a coincidence, but I believe it was March 5, 1957 (six years to the day Patsy would die in a plane crash near Camden, Tennessee). Patsy had to go to California for a couple of weeks so I took off work and went with her. Being drafted couldn't have come at a worse time. Instead of being with her while she was getting her career off the ground and divorcing Gerald Cline, I was in a series of army bases in the Carolinas and Georgia. With the exception of one weekend we spent together when she stopped off on her way to Florida, it was a long-distance romance."

While Charlie was undergoing basic training in the army at Fort Bragg, Patsy went back into the studio in Nashville on 23 May 1957 with Owen Bradley to record six follow-up singles to *Walkin' After Midnight* in the hope of duplicating its success — *I Don't Wanta, Ain't No Wheels On This Ship, That Wonderful Someone, I Can't Forget You, Hungry For Love*, and *(Write Me) In Care Of The Blues*. While these songs were being mastered, Decca released a 45 rpm record of two previous recordings, *Today, Tomorrow And Forever* and *Try Again*, whose titles had an uncanny link with Patsy's personal life as she was divorcing Gerald Cline and preparing to marry Charlie Dick. These songs would appear with *Walkin' After Midnight* on her first album, PATSY CLINE, released on 5 August 1957. For this work she would receive The Most Promising Country and Western Artist from *Billboard* magazine as well as the Greatest Achievements in Records Award for 1957 from *Music Vendor* magazine.

A month later on 8 September 1957 Patsy celebrated her twenty-fifth birthday, one week before her marriage to Charlie

Dick at her mother's new home in Winchester, an event Becky Green Miller recalls fondly. "My husband and I were at the wedding. The happiest day of Patsy' life was the day she married Charlie. I think the second happiest was when she had her first big hit. Talk about brides being radiant — she was shining. She had beautiful eyes and that day they just glittered. They were like stars."

BETSY
GREEN
MILLER

For the next year, Patsy and Charlie lived the typical life of newlyweds in the 1950s, moving into their army-base home at Fort Bragg and planning a family, as Charlie recalls. "As soon as we were married we took off for Fort Bragg. I didn't let the army slow us down. We hadn't planned a family but our daughter Julie snuck up on us anyway in August of '58. Patsy moved back with her mother because she didn't want to give birth in a military hospital. She wanted to be near her mother. For a couple of weeks after I got out of the army, Patsy and Julie and I stayed with her mother, then we found a small house, which we rented. I did odd jobs to make ends meet, but I knew we weren't going to be in Winchester very long. We stayed the summer of '59 and then decided it was time to move to Nashville."

Charlie delighted in getting the better of the U.S. Army. One of his favorite stories tells how he and Patsy were able to afford the move to Nashville. "When I got out of the army, a month early, Patsy was getting an allotment check of $137.00 a month and they still kept coming. We cashed the first one but didn't cash any more until we decided to move to Nashville. The only problem was we didn't have any money. We weren't doing too good because Patsy didn't have a hot record outside of *Walkin' After Midnight* and she wasn't on the Jimmy Dean show any more. She had worked a bit on another show with Don Owens in Washington, but it wasn't as big as the Dean show. We knew damn well the checks weren't ours but we ran to the bank and cashed them anyway.

CHARLIE
DICK

"We had barely got to Nashville when they came after us wanting to know where their money was. They wanted their money back. We had no money to pay them, so they set up a monthly pay-back deal. We paid them off. The money we came to

Nashville on was an over-payment from the Army."

During that two year period of time from late summer 1957, when Patsy and Charlie were married, to early summer 1959, when they moved to Nashville, Patsy returned to the recording studio eight times, still under the terms of her 4 Star contract, in search of a follow-up hit to *Walkin' After Midnight*, releasing such songs as *Just Out Of Reach* and *Try Again*. While these songs did not chart, she did try again on 27 January 1960 and again on 16 November 1960, when she recorded the Harlan Howard-Hank Cochran composition *I Fall To Pieces*. The song became her first Number 1 hit in the United States and Great Britain.

Date September 30, 1954

PATSY CLINE
Name of Artist

824-A East Patrick St.,
Address

Frederick, MD.

Dear Patsy Cline:

1. This contract for the personal services of musicians is made between Four Star Record Co. Inc. as the employer and you and the musicians who, from time to time during the term of this agreement, make up the orchestra represented by you as leader.

2. We hereby employ the personal services of you and such musicians individually, and you and such musicians will perform together for us under your leadership for the purpose of making phonograph records.

3. Recordings will be made at recording sessions, in our studios, at mutually agreeable times during the term hereof. A minimum of 16 78 r.p.m. record sides, or the equivalent thereof, shall be recorded during the period of this contract, and additional recordings shall be made at our election. The musical compositions to be recorded shall be mutually agreed upon between you and us, and each recording shall be subject to our approval as satisfactory, for manufacture and sale. As to each recording session a separate Form B contract, on the form then approved by the American Federation of Musicians of the United States and Canada (hereinafter called the "Federation") shall be entered into. No recording shall be made by dubbing.

4. We will pay you in respect of recordings made hereunder, a royalty of 2.34 % of the retail the country of manufacture of 90% of all records sold embodying performances hereunder one-half the thereof; pro centages eith for records retail list pr United State

5. F fourteen day cians in whe or at the rat earned. W

14. The period of this contract shall be two year(s) commencing with the date hereof.

15. The Federation will not approve any such agreement unless provision is made for the recording of at le eight (8) sides during each year of the term of the agreement.

16. The term of any agreement, including all options, cannot exceed three (3) years.

You grant us the option to renew this contract for a period of one year(s) upon all the terms a conditions herein contained, except for the option to renew for a further period. This option may be exercised us by giving you notice in writing at least thirty days prior to the expiration hereof; and such notice to you may given by delivery to you personally or by mailing to you at your address last known to us.

Very truly yours,

FOUR STAR RECORD COMPANY Inc.,

Employer

By _Wm. A. McCall Pres_

ACCEPTED

x _Patsy Cline_
Leader and Representatives of Employees

WITNESS: _Bill Peer_

Charles Town, W.Va.
Address:

Excerpts from Patsy's infamous contract with 4 Star Record Co. Inc.

Patsy performing on the set of the Arthur Godfrey Show, *1957.*

Owen Bradley (left) and Paul Cohen of Decca Records.

Patsy Cline and Charlie Dick celebrating their marriage, 15 September 1957.

Autographed publicity photo, 1957.

three

June 23/61

Dear Louise & All,

    I was sure glad to get your cards and letters, and even though I'm in bed in traction, I hope you'll be able to read this.

    Honestly, I've got so many calls, telegrams, cards & letters that I'm stunned. I didn't know there were so many people in this world who knew of me, but it sure gives me faith and a wonderful feeling to know so many fans and friends are wanting me to get well again.

    Plastic surgery will need to be done on me in three months. I don't think I'll ever be able to ride in a car again. I just thank God above that I can see perfectly and that my babies weren't with me. The doctors say I'll be home in twelve days and singing by the end of two months . . .

            Always
            Patsy

When Charlie and Patsy arrived in Nashville, courtesy of Uncle Sam, they rented a house on East Marthona Drive in Madison, just north of the city, across the street from Hank Snow's home, and renewed their acquaintance with old "Town and Country" and now Grand Ole Opry hillbilly friends Carl and Pearl Butler who introduced them to music city society at their Sunday get-togethers. Charlie found a job at the Curley Printing Company as a linotype operator, resuming the profession he left behind in Winchester, and Patsy headed back out on tour with the likes of Faron Young, who introduced her to his manager, Hubert Long, and his protege, Randy Hughes, a rhythm guitarist married to Katholoma "Kathy" Copas, daughter of Cowboy Copas. Hughes became Patsy's first real manager.

These first months in Nashville were not easy times for Patsy and Charlie, as he explains, though they were able to move from their East Marthona Drive home to a suburban neighborhood on Hillhurst Drive in northeast Nashville. "It was just after we moved onto Hillhurst Drive," Charlie recalls. "One night, when Patsy was on the road, I had Roger Miller and a couple of pickers over to the house. They were just jamming and having some beer. Somebody had to go and wake up Johnny Paycheck, who was Donny Young at the time, to go on the road with Ray Price. I volunteered because I wasn't a picker. I had a car accident on the way and was in the hospital for a while. I got out and we got very down. I couldn't work, and work wasn't that good for Patsy because she was pregnant with our son Randy. We had a car repossessed and just about everything that could happen to us did. Then the new contract came along about that time."

When Patsy had signed her first recording contract with 4 Star Records, she was just twenty-two and inexperienced. She didn't have a lawyer and didn't realize how restrictive the terms of the contract were. "When we came to Nashville, in August of '59," Charlie continues, "Patsy still had her 4 Star contract, which she signed September 30, 1954, and she could only record 4 Star songs. So far none of the songs had done anything outside of *Walkin' After Midnight*. I was a linotype operator and there was a

CHARLIE DICK

printing center so I got a job. That gave us eating money. The only work Patsy got was an occasional guest shot on the Opry — Friday night and two shots on Saturday night. She might have got $25.00. The only other work Patsy was getting was mostly on long tours. They didn't have interstates and people didn't run back home over the weekends. When you left, by God, you was gone! They were thirty to forty day tours and averaged between fifty to a hundred dollars a day. Expenses had to come out of that. We were really waiting, biding our time, for Patsy to get out of the 4 Star contract, which was coming to an end in 1960. Then, hopefully, we'd find somebody who would want to give her a better contract.

"If 4 Star had just let her do a couple of songs that she wanted to record, she would have been satisfied. Thinking back, I wonder why they didn't. If they had, they might have been able to con her into another contract. The biggest frustration for Patsy was having to record songs that she didn't feel comfortable with and know that if you did the best job you could, it was still going to be a mediocre record. We just had to wait it out. That was the only thing we could do.

"Prior to moving to Nashville the majority of work Patsy got was through the Hubert Long Agency," Charlie reports. "We hoped that Long would sign her but he wouldn't — or couldn't. Long only had two clients, country singers Ferlin Husky and Faron Young, and that was the way it was going to stay. We had met Randy Hughes at the Opry and on some of the tours. We became friends. He was a bit of a musician and picked with Ferlin and Faron. He was also learning the booking business through Hubert Long, and we knew that anybody connected with Long had learned right.

"The best part for Patsy was that she was his only client. It was slow at first but he got her booked on some of the better shows and tours, especially after she went with the other company, Decca Records, and had hit records. He put her in Vegas and there were very few country singers that had been in Vegas at that time. He worked awful hard for her."

Patsy did sign with Decca Records in 1960. Decca had recently appointed her long-time producer Owen Bradley to their A & R (artist and repertoire) position in Nashville. "When the 4 Star contract finished we found out that Decca would like to keep Patsy on as an artist, so we went and talked to Owen Bradley," Charlie explains. "He wanted Patsy, but he knew that because of her unhappy experience with 4 Star, she might think Decca was part of it and wouldn't want to stay." Such was not the case. Under contract with Decca and guided by the genius of Owen Bradley, Patsy soon had her first Number 1 hit with *I Fall To Pieces*, a song co-written by Hank Cochran and Harlan Howard.

OWEN BRADLEY

Owen Bradley was delighted that Patsy signed with Decca Records. "I thought she could go with any label that she wanted to and I was tickled to death that she wanted to stay." Charlie recounts the negotiation for an advance upon signing with typical Dick elan. "We were pretty far down and Patsy asked for a five hundred advance thinking that they may knock it down to four or three." Bradley was able to secure the advance from Decca head office in New York. "I called Decca and said that Patsy wanted a few dollars, an advance against royalties, it wasn't much. New York was also tickled that she wanted to stay. They sent her the money." As Charlie responds, he was grateful for the advance but wished Patsy had asked for more. "Hell, we got the money the next day. We probably could have got five thousand and didn't know it."

The recording of *I Fall To Pieces* by Patsy Cline happened more by default than by plan, as co-authors Hank Cochran and Harlan Howard recall, with contributions from Harlan's wife at the time, country singer Jan Howard. "It happened in the summer of 1960," Harlan Howard picks up the story of the song. "I had just moved to Nashville from California and Hank and I were writing for the same publishing company. Hank came by the house one day and says, hey, I got this little song going called *I Fall to Pieces*. I've only got a couple of lines but I've got a melody. He started to sing it.

HARLAN HOWARD

"I liked it. I didn't have a writing room because I was just renting the house, so we went out to the garage. I had a couple of old chairs and a table. We sat down and wrote the song. To be honest, it was just one song out of about fourteen we wrote in about three hours that day. It shows you how smart we were. The public tells you what are hits long afterwards. We just do the best we can. I am sure glad Hank came by that day."

Harlan's wife Jan was thrilled when Harlan and Hank told her *I Fall To Pieces* was her song. "Harlan, who was my husband at the time, and Hank called me out to the garage and sang *I Fall to Pieces* for me. I said hey, that's great. That's my song. They said this is your song. I was so thrilled. I made the demo on the song thinking it was for me."

It didn't take Owen Bradley long to realize *I Fall to Pieces* had everything necessary to become a hit. "We played Jan Howard's demo for Owen Bradley," Harlan recalls. "He thought it was a hit. Near as I can remember Patsy didn't like it, but she recorded it, and thank goodness she did."

Patsy was not Bradley's first choice to perform the song, however, nor was Jan Howard. Rather, he asked Roy Drusky to record *I Fall To Pieces*, which he declined to do. But Patsy was in the right place at the right time, as Drusky explains. "When I first met Patsy I was in Owen Bradley's office. He said 'I've got a hit song here. I want you to hear it.' He played *I Fall To Pieces* and I guess I didn't react the way he wanted me to.

"'Well what do you think,' asked Owen.

"'It's a good song.'

"'It's a great song.'

"'Ya, it's a great song but I really think it's a girl's song. It just isn't a boy's song.'

"Owen got a little upset and said, 'That's alright. You just don't record it. I'm going to record it with somebody else and it's going to be a Number 1 record.'

"I walked out of the office and Patsy was laying on the couch. If I remember right she had on light blue jeans.

"She said, 'Hi, you're Roy Drusky?'

"'Ya.'

"'I'm Patsy Cline.'

"I told her that was great, but I had never heard of Patsy Cline. I asked her if she was waiting to see Mr. Bradley.

"'I'm going to record for Decca,' she said.

JAN
HOWARD

ROY
DRUSKY

"I told her that was great because he's got a hit song for a girl. I told Owen he was right later on, but I wasn't wrong either because a girl did it. Didn't she?"

I Fall To Pieces

I fall to pieces
Each time I see you again,
I fall to pieces,
How can I be just your friend?
You want me to act like we've never kissed,
You want me to forget,
Pretend we've never met,
And I've tried and I've tried,
But I haven't yet.
You walk by and I fall to pieces.

(Lyrics by Hank Cochran and Harlan Howard, copyright 1960, Tree Publishing Co., Inc.)

RAY WALKER

I Fall To Pieces was recorded 16 November 1960 while Patsy was almost seven months pregnant and released on 30 January 1961, eight days after Patsy's son "Randy" was born. Patsy's joy at both events was evident to everyone, including Ray Walker, a member of The Jordanaires who had begun to provide vocal backing on Patsy's recordings. "Patsy got what she wanted — a hit. She came into the studio and said, 'Ray, honey! They can't take that refrigerator now, they'll never get my car now. I paid cash for them and they're mine and I'm keeping them.'

"I asked her were she got the money and Patsy said, 'Owen gave it to me 'cause baby I've got a hit record. I didn't get a dime off the last one (*Walkin' After Midnight*) but I'm getting paid for this one.'

"She was the happiest person, at the moment."

It took a long time before Jan Howard got over Harlan and Hank breaking their promise to her by giving *I Fall to Pieces* to Patsy. "Harlan came home and said guess who's going to record *I Fall to Pieces?*'

"I said, 'I am!'

"He said, 'Wrong, Patsy Cline is.'

"Well, it almost caused a divorce. He said just look and you know how many records you'd probably sell. He was right. He said Patsy could have a monster on this and it's for the family. I fell for it. I was glad afterwards because it really was Patsy's song. I couldn't have done the justice to it that she did.

"I remember something else about *I Fall To Pieces*. Freddy Hart had brought me a song called *Lovin' In Vain*. I wanted to record that song so bad it's a miracle that Patsy and I remained friends after all this. Joe Johnson was my producer at the time. I took it to Joe and he turned it down for me. It broke my heart. I said don't worry Freddy I'll get a record on this. I took it to Patsy and she loved it. She recorded the song and in fact I think she liked that song better than *I Fall To Pieces*. I don't think to this day Freddy has ever said thank you because *Lovin' In Vain* ended up being the 'B' side of *I Fall To Pieces*. Funny how things turn out."

JAN HOWARD

Jan Howard had been a Patsy Cline fan long before she started singing herself, long before Patsy recorded *I Fall To Pieces*, as she recalls. "I was living in California and had a top ten record at the time, so I was asked to appear on the Opry. Johnny Cash said, 'When you go to Nashville and do the Opry just do your spot and leave. Don't hang around 'cause that's when you get in trouble.' I don't know what trouble I was supposed to get into, but he was more an authority on that, I guess. I'd do my spot, and if Patsy was on I'd hang around so I could hear her sing. But I never met her 'cause I didn't have the courage to walk up and say, 'I'm Jan Howard and I've always been a fan.' As soon as she would sing I'd go back to the ladies' rest room and change clothes. I was back there changing one night when the door flew open and there stood Patsy in her cowgirl outfit, fringes, boots and everything. I was like WOW! It was like a giant had walked in.

"She put her hands on her hips and said, 'Well you're a conceited little son-of-a-bitch.'

"I said, 'What?'

"'You just waltz in here, do your spot and waltz out. You don't say hello or kiss my foot or anything to anybody.'

"I said, 'Now wait just a damn minute.' My Irish and Indian temper came up. 'I've always been a fan of yours but right now I'm not. Besides that, where I'm from when a stranger moves to town the people who live there make them feel welcome. There ain't a damn soul in this town who has made me feel welcome.'

"Boy she laughed. You could hear her a block away.

"'You're alright honey. Anybody that will talk back to the Cline is alright. We're going to be good friends.'"

"And we were. Suddenly, I wasn't afraid of Patsy Cline."

Another friend Patsy made backstage at the Grand Ole Opry was Dottie West. "I was backstage and walked up to her and said, 'I'm Dottie West and I'm the one that's been writing you fan letters. And I want to say that's the only fan letter I've ever written.' I was living in Cleveland and heard her on the Godfrey Show. She always answered her mail. Patsy loved to laugh and she laughed a lot. She had a hearty, big, laugh. Most all the time she was bubbly. I just loved to hear her laugh. You don't really hear a chuckle from Willie Nelson, you see him smile a lot. He's a happy person. To show you the comparison Patsy would really laugh out loud and it was fun. She was a fun person to be with."

Other country stars who toured with Patsy following the success of I Fall To Pieces have similar fond memories of her boisterous character and sensitive heart. Ferlin Husky tells a revealing tale about their tour to Pearl Harbor, Hawaii. "Patsy talked a lot when on stage. If anybody heckled her, she'd stop and tell them off. All the sailors were yelling and whistling and hollering for her to sing something. She sings a couple of songs then starts talking.

"She says, 'Next I'd like to do *Walkin' After Midnight*. It never went to Number 1 because I was underneath Ferlin Husky.'

"When you say something like that at a military base, they're going to roar.

"Patsy tried to straighten it out and said, 'What I meant was, Ferlin was on top.'

"She didn't get to say anything else. The guys were screaming and whistling at her. What she was trying to tell them was that my hit single *Since You've Gone* came out about the same time as *Walkin' After Midnight* and *Gone* was already ahead of *Walkin'* in

Billboard and *Cashbox*. Patsy got off stage and began crying. I really felt sorry for her. I told her to get right out there and start singing. She told them they had had their laugh, now it was her turn. She just tore them up."

Patsy did indeed have the last laugh, even on Ferlin Husky, when *I Fall To Pieces* entered the *Billboard* charts, both country and pop, on 3 April 1960, the second time she had scored on both charts after doing so in 1957 with *Walkin' After Midnight*. Throughout the spring, *I Fall To Pieces* rose steadily, hitting Number 1 on the country chart on August 7th and Number 12 on the pop chart on September 12th, ranking above Elvis Presley's *Little Sister* and Roy Orbison's *Crying* that week. *I Fall To Pieces* remained on the *Billboard* charts for 39 weeks. In the October issue of *Billboard*, Patsy was named in a country deejay poll the Favorite Female Vocalist in the country on the strength of *I Fall To Pieces*, then one month later she was named Most Programmed Female Vocalist in *Cashbox* and Female Vocalist of the Year in *Music Vendor*. Just as *I Fall To Pieces* began a slow descent on the charts, *Crazy*, released in mid-October, began its meteoric rise.

The success of *I Fall To Pieces* is somewhat ironic since Patsy claims to have never liked the song, as Owen Bradley explains. "I thought Patsy liked *I Fall To Pieces*. It was not until later, after recording session, that she told me she only did that one to please me. She liked the other side better (*Lovin' In Vain*). That's from her lips, not mine. I was very pleased that it turned out to be a hit."

Harlan Howard remembers when Patsy gave him a gift in appreciation for writing the song. "She had personally gone out and got me a bracelet. The engraving says, 'To Harlan. Thanks for the hit. Patsy.' I thought wow! This is nice. Singers give a present when you write them a hit. Thirty years later this is the only present that any singer ever gave me except a great recording. Now I know how special Patsy was."

The song remains one of the most dearly loved and widely covered songs in country music history and continues to influence women country artists today, such as Trisha Yearwood. "My favorite song that Patsy did is *I Fall To Pieces*," Trisha confesses.

"Harlan Howard is a friend of mine and I had him tell me all of the Patsy stories he could. Another song that really kills me is *Faded Love* because her version with the crack in her voice, at the end, makes it real, real human, which she had the ability to do like nobody else."

While Patsy's career headed for the stars, her domestic desires were also being fulfilled. She made fast friends with her neighbors, "Big Daddy" and Joyce Blair, nurtured her daughter Julie and newborn son Randy, and decorated her new home. "Big Daddy" Blair was one of the first neighbors to welcome Patsy and Charlie to the neighborhood when they moved into their new house on Hillhurst Drive. "I first met Patsy and Charlie when they moved into their new house. Of course, we went over to welcome them. Patsy always called me "Big Daddy" and would ask me for advice on anything. She asked, 'How do you know you are forgiven?' I told her, 'Patsy, the Bible says if you will ask in the name of the Lord, you will soon be forgiven. You have to believe and then you'll be forgiven. She was tickled to death to know that."

Joyce Blair was already a Patsy Cline fan when she moved in next door and became more than a neighbor — she became Patsy's domestic confidant and godmother to Julie and Randy. "I had heard Patsy sing on the Arthur Godfrey show and I loved her singing. It meant a lot to have her live in our neighborhood. We made it a point to go over, meet them, and invite them to our church. Patsy had a little girl, Julie, and we had a little boy, Kenny. They played in the backyard after they met. At that time Patsy was singing at the Opry on Saturday nights and doing some traveling, but not as much as she did later on. We had a chance to become good friends. She never called me Joyce. It was always 'Blair' and she always called my husband Big Daddy.

"Patsy had come from singing in a little church. She had it made for the rest of her life. But the Lord had different things for Patsy. I was more personal with her than with her work. To this day I've never heard anybody say that Patsy Cline wasn't one of the best that's ever been. Patsy hit the top and she will stay there. She's the best singer I've ever heard."

As Joyce recalls, life changed significantly in Patsy's household once *I Fall To Pieces* charted. "Patsy got back on her feet again and started to make money. I never will forget the new car that she got. It was a black and white Cadillac. That afternoon she comes screaming, 'Blair, come over here. Come here! I've got a new car.'"

Joyce also recalls the comedy of Randy's birth as Charlie refused to believe Patsy was in labor. Patsy couldn't wake up Charlie so she asked "Blair" to take her to the hospital. "The night came for the baby to be born and Charlie had been out all night, having himself a ball, I guess. Patsy couldn't get him awake so she came over and said, 'Blair it's time for the baby.' I ran and got the car. We took off for St. Thomas Hospital, and when we got to the entrance, my car stalled. I ran into the hospital, got a wheelchair, and got her to admitting."

CHARLIE
DICK

Somewhat embarrassed, Charlie tells his side of the story. "Patsy went to the doctor on Thursday and he told her she had about two more weeks. She said, 'Well, I'm set to do the Opry this weekend,' and he said, 'Go ahead and do it this weekend and that's it.' And that's how I almost missed Randy's birth because she did the Opry on Saturday night. I worked overtime that night and didn't go to the Opry. After we got through work we started playing poker and had a few beers. I stayed out all night. It might have been six when I got home and went to bed. No big deal. About seven o'clock Patsy came in trying to wake me up. She said she had to go to the hospital, she had labor pains. I said, 'Ya!' In my mind I was thinking she was just trying to get me up 'cause she's mad 'cause I had been out all night. Being as far along as she was she wasn't too comfortable either in bed together, but I wouldn't get up.

I remember one of the Blairs being in the house and I thought they had planned this together. I still didn't get up. Later, everything got real quiet so I got up and looked around, nobody was there, everybody was gone. Blair's husband told me that they had gone to the hospital. I jumped into the car. I almost missed Randy's birth."

With a hit song and a new son, the future was bright and life was great for Patsy and Charlie until Patsy was nearly killed in a car accident in front of Madison High School on 14 June 1961. "I was back on my feet and back to work and Patsy had got some work with *I Fall to Pieces*," Charlie recalls. "Things were starting to pick up. Then, all of a sudden, Patsy had a car accident. Patsy and her brother Sam had gone to Madison to do grocery shopping. They were coming back across Old Hickory Boulevard which, at that time, was a two lane road. It was late in the afternoon and rainy. A car in the opposite direction, pulled out to pass, and hit the car Patsy and her brother Sam were in head-on. Patsy went through the windshield. Her injuries were serious — a broken hip, broken wrist, and severe facial lacerations. Sam had his chest punctured by the horn ring on the steering wheel. Two passengers in the other car were killed."

Patsy, too, was in critical condition, as Joyce Blair recognized when she arrived at the hospital. "The next day when Patsy woke up they let me go in. Of course, Charlie had been in. I went to her bedside. She reached over and got my hand and said Blair, Jesus has been in my room. He has taken my hand and told me, 'Not now. I have other things for you to do.' She said she knew it was the Lord because He came in with a big brightness."

JOYCE
BLAIR

Patsy's remarkable experiences in the hospital were magnified when she heard a young woman on the radio singing *I Fall To Pieces* in her honor. The young woman was Loretta Lynn who performed the tribute on Ernest Tubb's *Midnight Jamboree* following the Grand Ole Opry. Patsy immediately sent Charlie out to find Loretta on that late Saturday night, as he recalls. "It was a Saturday night while Patsy was in hospital that she sent me out to find Loretta Lynn. Patsy told me that there was a little girl who had sang *I Fall to Pieces* for her that night. She told me to go find her and tell her that she'd like to meet her. I went down to Tootsies but I didn't see any stranger. I went across the street to the Ernest Tubb Record Shop and went backstage — Tubb had his own radio show out of the back of the store following the Opry on WMS Radio. There was one person in there in western clothes. I went up to her and asked, 'Are you Loretta Lynn?'

'She said, "Yeah!'

"'I'm Charlie Dick. I'm Patsy Cline's husband.' Before I could say anything else she grabbed me around the neck. I thought she was going to break it. She called Mooney over and introduced him. We became good friends. I didn't get a chance to say what I wanted to say. She was too busy talking to me. Finally I said, Patsy's in the hospital and she would like to see you. Well, that just thrilled her to death."

LORETTA
LYNN

For her part, Loretta Lynn will never forget meeting Patsy in the hospital. A deep friendship began which Loretta still treasures. "Patsy's whole head was bandaged up. You could just see one eye. Her leg was hanging from the ceiling. She was in bad shape. We talked about things and she got a little bit sentimental. She started to cry and I could see a tear come out of this one eye. I never forgot that. I think about it often.

"When Ernest Tubb let me sing *I Fall To Pieces*, it was the first time that I got to sing in Nashville. I didn't know the song, so Mooney held the song book for me and I dedicated it to Patsy 'cause they told me she would be listening. She heard me and that was one of the reasons why a tear came down. She was thanking me.

"Me and Patsy became close friends right off. It seemed like we'd known each other before, but we never had. There were lots of times that Patsy didn't have anything and Patsy remembered this. She would give me things. She gave me clothes, I've still got. I still wear the earrings that Patsy gave me. She gave me underclothes. If it hadn't been for her. I wouldn't have no clothes, hardly."

JOYCE
BLAIR

When Patsy got on her feet, she wanted everybody else up there with her, as Joyce Blair comments upon Patsy's generosity. "I will never forget her doing all that shopping 'cause Loretta didn't have any curtains for her house. I remember Patsy buying stuff for the house and putting up her draperies for her. 'Til the day she died she never quit giving, she never quit loving."

Patsy's return to the Grand Ole Opry stage in August was as emotional as it was triumphant, as Ray Walker of The Jordanaires remembers. "When Patsy was well enough to get out of the hospital, they brought her to the Opry and wheeled her out on stage.

She was still bandaged in some areas, she was still bruised, she was in a wheel chair, and she couldn't walk. Those people stood for nearly five minutes and applauded that girl."

In Dottie West's opinion, Patsy's accident became a turning point in her career. "She was so determined, and of such strong character, that the accident wouldn't have stopped her. Just to get well and get back to work was wonderful. She fought it. The way it turned out Patsy was a lot prettier even after the accident. Although she had some scars she was prettier. She came back with a determination to lose weight. Her mother made her a different style of dress to wear on stage, and she started to buy some beautiful chiffons." Patsy Cline picked up the pieces and soon became the most famous woman country singer in the world with the release of *Crazy*.

RAY
WALKER

DOTTIE
WEST

Patsy's homes in Madison, Tennessee, at 213 East Marthona Drive (top), from 1959–61, and at 3024 Hillhurst Drive (opposite), from 1961–62. Patsy with Julie, Randy, and Charlie at home on Hillhurst Drive (bottom).

Patsy posing with (left to right) Owen Bradley, Randy Hughes, Justin Tubb, and Hank Cochran.

...... *Presenting*

Patsy Cline

THE AIM OF EVERY PERSON IN ANY PROFESSION IS TO BE RECOGNIZED AS "TOPS" IN HIS OR HER FIELD. THIS IS THE ULTIMATE, AND ONLY A FEW REACH THIS GOAL. PATSY CLINE HAS MADE IT. FOR SOME THIS ACCOMPLISHMENT CAME FAST AND EASY, BUT THIS ISN'T TRUE IN PATSY'S CASE.

HER LIFE BEGAN IN THE HEART OF THE SHENANDOAH VALLEY, NEAR WINCHESTER, VIRGINIA, AND HER PARENTS, MR. AND MRS. SAM HENSLEY NEVER FAILED TO GIVE PATSY THEIR HELP AND ENCOURAGEMENT. MRS. HENSLEY IS DECEASED NOW, BUT MRS. HENSLEY STILL PLAYS A VERY IMPORTANT ROLE IN PATSY'S CAREER, AS EVERYONE CAN SEE WHEN SHE STEPS TO THE STAGE DISPLAYING THE BEAUTIFUL DRESSES MADE BY HER.

WINNING A TAP DANCING CONTEST IN LEXINGTON, VIRGINIA AT THE AGE OF FOUR WAS THE BEGINNING IN SHOW BUSINESS FOR PATSY. THIS LED TO MANY OTHER CONTESTS AND OTHER FIRST PRIZES, AND AT THE AGE OF FIFTEEN SHE BEGAN REGULAR RADIO APPEARANCES WHICH CONTINUED UNTIL SHE FINISHED HIGH SCHOOL. THEN CAME A SERIES OF CLUB ENGAGEMENTS, OTHER RADIO AND TELEVISION APPEARANCES, AND A RECORDING CONTRACT ON A SMALL LABEL.

IN 1955, WITH A BAND FROM MARTINSBURG, VIRGINIA, PATSY AUDITIONED FOR THE "ARTHUR GODFREY TALENT SCOUTS SHOW." THEY ACCEPTED HER, BUT NOT THE BAND, SO SHE REGRETFULLY HAD TO REFUSE THE SHOW. SHE TRIED AGAIN UNSUCCESSFULLY IN 1956, AND FINALLY WON IN 1957 SINGING "WALKING AFTER MIDNIGHT." THE SONG WAS RECORDED, AND HAS SOLD OVER 1½ MILLION RECORDS. MR. GODFREY WAS VERY IMPRESSED WITH PATSY AND FOR TWO YEARS HAD HER AS A REGULAR ON HIS SHOW.

WITH THE HELP OF HER FRIEND AND MANAGER, RANDY HUGHES, PATSY BECAME A REGULAR MEMBER OF THE "GRAND OLE OPRY" IN 1960, AND ALSO SIGNED AN EXCLUSIVE CONTRACT WITH DECCA RECORDS. HER FIRST BIG RECORD FOR THEM WAS "I FALL TO PIECES", A SONG WHICH REALLY ESTABLISHED PATSY AS A RECORDING ARTIST.

JUST AT THE TIME "I FALL TO PIECES" WAS BEGINNING TO HIT ACROSS THE COUNTRY, SHE WAS SERIOUSLY INJURED IN AN AUTOMOBILE ACCIDENT, WHICH HOSPITALIZED HER FOR SEVERAL WEEKS. BUT WITH CONSTANT DETERMINATION, THE PRAYERS OF HER FAMILY AND FRIENDS, AND OVER 4,000 CARDS AND LETTERS, SHE WAS SOON OUT TOURING THE COUNTRY ON CRUTCHES. THE SONG BEGAN TO HIT EVERYWHERE, BOTH ON THE COUNTRY AND POP CHARTS, AND WENT ON TO BECOME THE #1 RECORD IN THE COUNTRY. HER FOLLOW-UP WAS "CRAZY", ANOTHER BALLAD, AND AT ONE TIME SHE HAD THE #1 AND #2 BEST SELLING SONG IN THE NATION. IN THE MEANTIME, THE CONSTANT DEMAND FOR HER SONGS LED DECCA TO RELEASE HER FIRST ALBUM, "PATSY CLINE SHOWCASE," WHICH IMMEDIATELY BECAME A "BEST SELLER". "SHE'S GOT YOU" FOLLOWED, AND PATSY CLINE WAS A PERSONALITY KNOWN FROM COAST TO COAST, AND SHE CONSTANTLY IN DEMAND FOR BOTH COUNTRY AND POP SHOWS.

HER MANY TV APPEARANCES INCLUDE: "THE DICK CLARK SHOW", "AMERICAN BANDSTAND", "THE PHILIP MORRIS SHOW", AND "JUBILEE USA". SHE HAS PLAYED TO AUDIENCES ALL ACROSS THE COUNTRY INCLUDING APPEARANCES IN NIGHT CLUBS, STAGE SHOWS, AND MADE ONE APPEARANCE IN CARNEGIE HALL. SHE HAS RECEIVED MANY AWARDS, THE MOST COVETED ONE BEING VOTED "FAVORITE FEMALE VOCALIST", IN THE BILLBOARD MAGAZINE COUNTRY DISC JOCKEY POLL.

THIS IS HER STORY..... MANY CHAPTERS HAVE ALREADY BEEN WRITTEN AND MANY MORE ARE BEING WRITTEN DAILY. FOR EACH DAY BRINGS A NEW AND MORE EXCITING CHAPTER IN THE LIFE AND CAREER OF PATSY CLINE.

Exclusive Management

RANDY HUGHES AGENCY

4415 GRA MAR DRIVE • NASHVILLE, TENNESSEE • TELEPHONE CAnal 8-2242

★ GRAND OLE OPRY TALENT ★

Patsy rehearsing with Ernest Tubb (center) circa 1961.

four

CRAZY

Patsy's publicity photo for Arthur Godfrey's Talent Scouts.

September 10, 1962

Dear Anne:

I just got in from Minnesota where I worked a show last night in pouring rain. The damn fool people sat right out in it and yelled for more. Over five thousand of them. They must have been either crazy or nuts over country, is all I can say. I'll see you in Toronto on the 13th of October and in Hamilton on the 18th.

I have to go to Vegas for five weeks starting November 23rd to December 27th. Yeah! Christmas too. I could cuss everybody out there for that booking.

Well I've got to get the little apes to bed. I feel like hell with a cold after that wet show last night.

Tell everyone hello and don't buy my new album. I'll send you one. I just cut eight sides which will make four new records and one should be out in three to four weeks.

Well, I'll see you soon, might even bring that crazy Charlie with me.

Love always,
Patsy

T wo months after her near fatal automobile accident, Patsy Cline was performing weekly again at the Grand Ole Opry, albeit in a wheel chair at first, then supported by a cane. As Jordanaire and Opry regular Ray Walker remembers, "She got well again and she had some work done on her face. Then she came back after she got completely well and just knocked the Opry out. I believe it was Roy Acuff she was on with and he just let her sing two or three numbers, whatever she wanted to sing. She was slim again, walkin' tall.

RAY
WALKER

"She said, 'Looky here, I've got me some four-inch heels. I'm going to Hollywood baby but I'm still country.'" Patsy would indeed take "country" to Hollywood by way of Carnegie Hall and Las Vegas over the next two years, helping to establish country music in the firmament of contemporary American popular culture.

That same August Patsy was back in the studio recording again, with The Jordanaires backing her vocals, which, according to Jordanaire Neil Matthews Jr., were stronger than ever. "She came back like this wasn't going to get her down, and boy she was back with exuberance and ready to go. She probably did some of her best recording after the accident." On 17 August 1961, Patsy recorded *The Wayward Wind*, one of Charlie Dick's favorites. "Patsy didn't listen to any pop and she wasn't crazy about doing a pop song. Then she took *The Wayward Wind*, which was not really a country song, and it came out great. I think that's one of the best records she ever cut."

The Wayward Wind

Oh, the wayward wind is a restless wind,
A restless wind that yearns to wander,
And I was born the next of kin,
The next of kin to the wayward wind.
In a lonely shack by a railroad track
I spent my younger days,
And I guess the sound of the outward bound,
Made me a slave to wandrin'.

NEIL
MATTHEWS
JR

(Lyrics by Herb Newman and Stan Lebowsky,
copyright 1955, Polygram International Publishing, Inc.)

During this session in the studio, Patsy also recorded *Strange* by Mel Tillis, which he had intended for the Everly Brothers. Patsy recorded this Tillis song on 25 August 1961, a recording that has become a rarity and a collector's item. "I wrote *Strange* in Nashville," Tillis explains, "and at that time songs were coming to me just boom, boom, boom, boom. I seemed to think they were blessings. I looked up there one day and there was *Strange* and I got it. It was co-written with Fred Burch — it's been a good song. I wrote it originally for the Everly Brothers and I had a demo. It had the Everly sound. I went over to the studio one day, and Patsy was recording. I sang it to her in person. She said, 'I like that.' She cut it."

Strange

Strange, how you stopped lovin' me,
How you stopped needing me when she came along.
Oh, how strange.
Oh, how strange.
Well, I guess that I was just a puppet
You held on a string.
To think I thought you really loved me.
But look what thoughts can bring.
Strange, you're still in all my dreams.
Oh, what a funny thing:
I still care for you.
Oh, how strange.

(Lyrics by Mel Tillis and Fred Burch,
copyright 1961, Clearwood Publishing)

MEL
TILLIS

A few days earlier, though, Patsy recorded a song that would not become a rarity, but rather would make a young songwriter named Hugh Nelson into a celebrity. Tootsie, the proprietor of the Orchid Lounge, Charlie Dick's favorite hangout, introduced Charlie to Hugh "Willie" Nelson, an aspiring young songwriter who had recently arrived in Nashville looking for work. Hank Cochran later brought to Charlie a demo for the song Nelson called *Crazy*, but Patsy wouldn't listen to it when Charlie played it for her. "I was on the way to work one afternoon and stopped in for a beer at Tootsie's," Charlie picks up the story. "Mel Tillis was there. We were sitting in a booth and a record came on. It was a good one but we had no idea who it was. Tootsie said, 'It's Hugh Nelson, his wife works next door.' We didn't know Hugh Nelson. Patsy and I were at the Opry the following Saturday night and I sent one of the gophers to the tuck shop to buy me the record Mel and I heard the week before in Tootsie's. He came back and said it wasn't available. I went and saw Tootsie and she said for me to come upstairs with her. She said, 'Here's Hugh Nelson.' He told me that he'd just gotten to town and was broke. I told him I really liked his record but couldn't buy it. He told me he had one in his car and went to get it for me. It was *Night Life* and *Rainy Day Blues*. After we got home I laid down in front of the juke box we had and listened to it half the night. It didn't make Patsy too happy.

"A day or so later I ran into Hank Cochran and told him about Patsy being unhappy 'cause I stayed up all night listening to Willie's record. A couple of days later Hank came around with a tape. It was *Crazy*. I loved it as soon as I heard it. Patsy didn't want to hear it because she was still mad at me for playing Willie's record all night. When Patsy finally listened to the demo, she didn't like it. Willie almost talked the song instead of singing it. She still listened to it but didn't like it. Learning the song was the part she hated most. I told Hank I'd get it to Owen Bradley. Between us we conned her into recording it."

CHARLIE
DICK

Crazy

Crazy, crazy for feeling so lonely,
I'm crazy, crazy for feelin' so blue.
I knew you'd love me as long as you wanted,
And then someday you'd leave me for somebody new.
Worry, why do I let myself worry.
Wondrin' what in the world did I do?
Crazy for thinking my love could hold you,
I'm crazy for tryin', crazy for cryin',
And I'm crazy for lovin' you.

(Lyrics by Willie Nelson,
copyright 1961, Tree Publishing Co., Inc.)

For Hugh "Willie" Nelson, Patsy's recording of his song was the big break he was seeking when he moved to Nashville. *Crazy* was released on 16 October 1961, two months after Patsy recorded it, an event Willie recalls. "When I found out there was a possibility of Patsy Cline doing a Willie Nelson song, that really set me up. Every female vocalist in the world would like to have had a voice like Patsy Cline because everyone I've talked to, or seen, or heard, they're Patsy Cline fans. Patsy Cline had more woman fans than most women singers. All the girls like her and all the men like her. Patsy Cline had such an unique, such a good voice that naturally everyone who heard it did a double take. It's been said a million times. There's only one Patsy Cline. She was good, she was more than good. There was something that set her apart and you can't describe it. I can't.

"Patsy Cline's recording of *Crazy* was my favorite, all time, song of mine that anyone ever did. Patsy Cline singing *Crazy* was just a lot of magic."

Owen Bradley would be the first to concur with Willie on the "magic" of *Crazy*. "Thank God for *Crazy* because I think that's probably the best country song that I ever had anything to do with. New York had said, 'Can you do something a little more pop because *I Fall To Pieces* was too country.' Twenty-five years later we're doing the same thing. I think this is the reason I liked that record because I felt we did kind of walk the line."

Singing *Crazy* was not an easy task for Patsy, though, in part because of the lingering effects of her accident, as Bradley recalls. "So here we are in the studio and Patsy can't sing. She can't hit this one note because her rib cage had been injured and was so sore. Three hours is up and we're still working and she's saying, 'I can't get it!' She was beating on herself. Finally I said, 'Patsy there's no point in abusing yourself, don't try any more.'"

That evening Charlie and Patsy worked out the way to approach the song, the Cline way. "Patsy was trying to do it phrase by phrase like Willie had on the demo," Charlie explains. "After we come home that night she listened to the track and went back the next day and sang it straight and did it in two takes."

"I felt that Patsy really went through a lot to get that song,"

WILLIE NELSON

OWEN BRADLEY

80

Owen Bradley remarks, appreciatively. "It's been wonderful."

Other country performers also attest to the magic and wonder of *Crazy*, such as country music star Jim Glaser of the The Glaser Brothers. "*Crazy* is a beautifully written song, the song of Patsy's that's always been my favorite. It seems to be one of those songs that were written for her particular voice, even though it may not have been. What she did with those songs was so special that I always had the feeling that they would never have been quite as big a hit as they were had she not recorded them and given them her personal interpretation."

Crazy remains one of Eddy Arnold's favorite songs, as well. "I always play *Crazy*. It has a wide range and she could hit that low note and she could hit the high note. My goodness the woman was a great singer." Harold Bradley ranks *Crazy* near the top of his all-time country hit list. "I've been in the music business a long time. That particular song is one of my favorites of all the songs I've heard — and I've heard a lot of songs." And as Ronna Reeves notes, the song has become a mainstay of country acts. "I worked in nightclubs and that's one of the most requested songs. If you don't sing *Crazy*, well — then you're crazy."

Crazy rose to Number 1 on the *Billboard* country charts and Number 9 on the pop charts, another "crossover" achievement to rank just ahead of *I Fall To Pieces* and *Walkin' After Midnight* on the "Cline" career chart. During the 1962 awards season, Patsy received the *Music Reporters'* Award as well as the Favorite Female Artist Award and Star of the Year Award, based on the success of *Crazy* and her follow-up hit, *She's Got You*.

Much of the studio success of songs like *Crazy* and *I Fall To Pieces* came from the creative heat generated by the interplay between the respective genius of Owen Bradley and Patsy Cline, as Jordanaire Neil Matthews Jr. and others testify. "Most of the girl singers The Jordanaires worked with were 'yes sir' and 'no sir.' Patsy came in to a session and it wasn't 'yes sir' and 'no sir.' It was give and take between her and Owen. She came on like gang busters and Owen came on like gang busters."

Adds session guitarist Harold Bradley, Owen's brother, "we looked forward to the fight between Patsy and my brother. They

JIM
GLASER

EDDY
ARNOLD

HAROLD
BRADLEY

RONNA
REEVES

NEIL
MATTHEWS
JR

definitely argued in the beginning of the session about how they wanted to do this and how they wanted to do that 'cause she had her ideas on how she wanted to do it. Here she's dealing with a tremendous musician and it was a matter of them kind of getting some kind of compromise. We always thought it was getting her singing until she got a little bit tired. The first hour, we knew, was going to be a war until all of a sudden, when they found the formula, everybody was happy. As soon as Owen and Patsy had hits, they didn't have any more arguments, but that's something my brother won't really talk about."

HAROLD BRADLEY

As Hank Cochran observed, Patsy and Owen would lock horns but somehow they worked it out. "They clashed hard at times. I know that on one of my songs, *You're Stronger Than Me*, they really had a difference of opinion. In fact, they cut it in two different ways — one time with strings and then they cut it with a kind of like *I Fall To Pieces* feel. She had her own ideas."

You're Stronger Than Me

If you're sincere when you say you don't care
That our love is just a memory,
If you can have fun with some other one,
Darling, you're stronger than me.
For if still loving you means I'm weak,
Then I'm weak, for I still fall apart
When you speak or we meet.
If the love that we knew won't bother you,
Darling, you're stronger than me.

(Lyrics by Hank Cochran and Jimmy Key, copyright 1961, Tree Publishing Co., Inc.)

HANK COCHRAN

And as Charlie Dick observed in more than one session, Patsy and Owen were not above trading off songs so that, in the end, both got their way. "Patsy and Owen had a friendly feud going. Owen had a lot of songs he wanted to record, but she didn't want to. She had songs that she wanted to record and Owen didn't. So they would trade out. She once told Owen that she wanted to cut *Faded Love* without modulating her voice. She recorded that just for spite to show Owen that she could record it without modulating.

"There is a Floyd Tillman song called *I Love You So Much It Hurts*, one of the greatest songs ever written. There's a note in there that goes down below these chairs and when she got ready to record one of the musicians says, 'Okay, what key? She hollered a key and Owen said, 'No! We won't use that key.' He said a girl doesn't sing that low. Patsy said, 'I do.' Owen said, 'Well if you think you can, then go ahead. Run through it boys.' They went through one time and he's thinking she wouldn't make it. Well, she did and after that they never argued about keys again.

CHARLIE DICK

"One time Owen brought up a song which I dearly love, *Does Your Heart Beat For Me*." Patsy had never heard of it. God, I thought everybody had heard it. It was Russ Morgan's theme song. Patsy wasn't crazy about doing it until after she recorded it. It was good."

"Tennessee Ploughboy" Eddy Arnold praises Owen Bradley's ability to inspire artists to achieve their potential, especially women artists. "Owen had a great way of producing lady singers — some people can some can not. He could. He had great success with girl singers like Patsy, Brenda Lee, and Loretta Lynn. He just had that little touch of picking the right song and mixing the record. A lot of people don't know what you mean when you say mixing the recording. That's editing. Owen had that and of course he happened to have some good talent.

"Where there's a very good singer who really captivates the audience, there will be other singers coming along that will be influenced by them. Patsy had the style and the charisma and the sound. She had it all. My gosh, that woman could sing. She could sing anything. She could sing country, she could sing pop, she could sing jazz. She could do anything. Oh yeah!"

EDDIE ARNOLD

Patsy wasn't the only singer to cross swords with Owen. Jan Howard had her moments. "Owen wasn't country, he was an orchestra leader and an excellent musician. He had a feel for songs, and I think if he believed in a song or an artist, then he would try to steer them in a way he thought they should go. He and I clashed quite a bit. I'm sure with Patsy's temperament — and

Owen's — they had their moments, too. But, that's business and when you're in that situation nobody is going to agree one hundred percent on anything. I think Owen would push you to your limit."

Owen Bradley was explosive when he wanted to make a point, Ray Walker recalls, but also a diplomat. "I don't think any other producer in Nashville could have handled Patsy the way Owen handled her. Owen could handle a situation that disrupted a session the best of any producer I know. With Patsy the marriage was beautiful, the blend was beautiful, and it worked perfectly. They came out with a product that was unbelievable and when they got through everybody was happy."

In Bill Anderson's opinion, no other producer he has known would have had the knack for pushing Patsy to the limit and getting the best out of her. "With no disrespect to anybody else, I think that Owen Bradley was the Patsy Cline 'sound.' I think he sensed the type of artist he had. Owen was very fond of Patsy personally and professionally. I think it showed in the records that he cut. He took the extra time — extra care. He saw the same kind of broad market appeal that maybe he saw in Brenda Lee and some of the other people he was producing who knew no boundaries with their music. You listen to Patsy's records today and you realize Owen cut them for the ages. You don't say, well that sounds like 1959, or that sounds like 1960. It sounds just great."

Loretta Lynn recalls the somewhat playful disputes between Patsy and Owen concerning her desire to yodel. "Patsy loved to yodel — that was funny — and Owen couldn't keep her from yodeling. She'd come in and say, 'I want to yodel, I want to yodel.' But Owen kept telling her, 'Patsy, don't yodel on these songs 'cause this is not the time.' Every now and then we'd have a laugh about it." As Bradley adds, "Maybe Patsy had a right to yodel on some of the material we had. Maybe we should have yodeled and growled a little more. It's true. Some of the early country singers did yodel. Some of the cowgirls, almost all of the cowgirls yodel, and some of the singers would growl. If they really felt that they weren't making it, they'd just put a little growl in their voice. I didn't particularly like that and used to have a few discussions about that. I used to think I won pretty good, but I still hear a little growl and a little bitty yodel now and then. It kind of worked out pretty good. As long as the public liked it, that's what we both were looking for."

As far as Owen himself was concerned, stories of a stormy relationship between Patsy and him were grossly exaggerated. "The relationship that I had with Patsy was not a stormy one. It was not like what was shown in the movie *Sweet Dreams*. It was not like the relationship she had with Charlie Dick. We weren't fighting all the time. Most of the time I saw her in my office and we had a very cordial relationship. We had great respect, each for the other — at least I like to feel it that way — and there's really nobody to dispute it. I'm the only one. I'll just leave it at that. I certainly had great respect for her and I'm very proud and feel very lucky to have had the opportunity to work with such a great artist."

OWEN BRADLEY

From time-to-time Patsy's professional relationship with Owen Bradley spilled over into her personal relationship with Charlie Dick. Charlie recalls one day when Owen kicked him out of the studio for distracting Patsy from the pain she was putting into her singing. "Patsy had a way of putting herself into a song. She lived the song. What she was singing about was happening in her mind, some way, some place. When I worked at the printing company, I was only four blocks away from the recording studio. I went in one night, and when you went to the door to the studio, you passed the control room before you got to where the artist was. Patsy was rehearsing a song.

"Owen called me into the control room. He said, 'Did you and Patsy have a fight today, or an argument?'

"I said, 'No, not any more than usual. Everything was great.'

Owen said, 'Well I want you to get out of here.'

"'I've only got a few minutes,' I tell him. 'I'm on my lunch break.'

"He said, 'Patsy's crying on every song, tears are running down her cheeks.' Owen said he didn't want her to see me. He seemed to think that maybe she was singing these songs and thinking about a little rift that we had before. He ran me out of

CHARLIE DICK

the studio. I think that it was just how deep she got into a song when she performed it."

PC

Much has been conjectured about the relationship Patsy had with her husband Charlie Dick, conjecture that has been turned into melodrama, if not soap opera, by Hollywood scriptwriters and New York biographers. But as Dottie West comments, "there was so much love there. They had their little differences like all couples do. It was sort of fun to watch when they'd get into little arguments because you knew Patsy was going to win. She had good control and yet she could really let Charlie be a man. She respected him that way too. He was her lover. He was her man. There was no doubt about it. When they would have a problem, I'd see her cry a bit like all us big girls do sometimes. You could see that it was just for pure love. She loved him to death."

Loretta Lynn compares her relationship with her husband Mooney, affectionately known as Doo, with Patsy's relationship with Charlie. "I love Charlie. Charlie was always fair. Charlie and Patsy would fight and quarrel like Doo and I. It was no big deal. They'd get mad and then Patsy would say, 'Boy, this is it. I've had it.' Charlie and Patsy was like me and Doo when it came to fighting. Patsy's husband, Charlie Dick, is a great person. I've always loved Charlie and I never knew of any problems between Charlie and Patsy that they didn't patch up within ten minutes after they had a fight, you know a quarrel about something, not a fight a quarrel. He's been my friend, always. He was the one that come and got me to meet Patsy. He'll always be my friend, he's great."

Charlie sets the record straight about what really happened one time when Patsy had him arrested and what he thinks of a couple of books that have been written about Patsy which have exaggerated their domestic quarrels. "We were both very strong minded, hard headed, whatever you want to call it. We didn't back down from each other a hell of a lot. We did argue quite a bit but it moved fast — it ended as fast as it started and it was forgotten. We didn't go around carrying a chip on our shoulder. If a stranger

DOTTIE
WEST

LORETTA
LYNN

walked in a door and didn't know what was going on, he might think we were going after the shotguns. None of that ever happened.

"We had a couple of little problems and one time she got hysterical and I smacked her. She called the law on me and I spent a few hours in jail. The judge made her come to court and drop it so I got my revenge right there, I got it right back. Some of the books that have been written about Patsy I think she would think are hilarious. There are a couple out now. One of them, I understand, is quoting the people who were in the airplane with her — they're all dead now. I'm going to find out where he got those quotes because I might want to talk to them myself.

"But the other stuff, there was fire between us. It made it awful good to make up and gave us a lot of time to do it."

Patsy's friend Del Wood didn't like the movie *Sweet Dreams* either because she felt the facts were distorted as far as Patsy and Charlie were concerned and missed capturing, by a country mile, what the real Patsy Cline was really like. "I'd like to say something about that movie. I did not like the way that Patsy and Charlie were portrayed. One of the things that Patsy and I shared was the fact that we both had a lot of problems in our marriages. If hers had been as bad as mine, she would have done the same thing I did, and that's get out of it. And Charlie, I've known Charlie for years. He couldn't have done to Patsy what that movie portrayed because if he had, there wouldn't have been a grease spot left of him. She would of really cleaned his clock. She really loved people — sure you love your family — but she loved people, and it breaks my heart that they didn't bring out this side of her, also some of the problems she had in the industry. We've all had problems but the love of the music industry is such that you almost have to love it better than anything or anybody in order to stay in it — to withstand the hardships that go along with it."

With the release of *Crazy*, *Strange*, *The Wayward Wind*, and other songs on her second album, SHOWCASE (WITH THE JORDANAIRES), released 27 November 1961, Patsy became a headline act, joining country stars Minnie Pearl, Jim Reeves, Faron Young, Bill Monroe, and Grandpa Jones for the first country music concert

DEL WOOD

87

at Carnegie Hall on 29 November 1961, which was graced with rave reviews in the New York papers. For Patsy, this was one of the highlights of her career and a benchmark in the history of country music, as she suggested in a letter to a friend.

October, 1961

Dear Mary,

On the 29th of November I'll be in Carnegie Hall in New York, eight men acts and myself and Minnie Pearl are the only ones (female) to go for the Opry Show, for the first time in history. How about that? Country music sure is in high cotton now.

Please forgive me if I can't write always but I'm always thinking of you. Write soon and take care, tell all hello.

Love,
Patsy

On a subsequent tour of Canada, Patsy met her soon-to-be close friend and pen pal Annie Armstrong from Guelph, Ontario, as Charlie Dick recalls. "Patsy comes back from Canada telling me about all these nice ladies that she had met. They went out and had dinner and a few drinks and did this and did that. I said, oh ya! Where were their husbands if they were such nice ladies? Oh, they were working. They don't like country music much anyhow. And, I said, ya, a nice bunch of ladies running all the time when their husbands are working — just raising hell. Patsy told Annie what I said. Annie said that the next time she played Canada she was to bring me and they'll bring their husbands. I came with Patsy, the husbands went to the show, and we became friends."

Patsy's next conquest would be playing Las Vegas over the Christmas season 1962–63. As Annie Armstrong recalls, "in those days it was something to get to Vegas and the money was something that Patsy had never heard of before. She had a hard row to hoe, four shows a night seven nights a week. It was hard on her but I do think she was proud as punch." Patsy was obviously thrilled about the way her career was going but it was hard work — traveling, personal appearances, recording sessions, two children, a home, and a husband.

ANNIE ARMSTRONG

Patsy on stage with Jim Reeves and Grandpa Jones.

Grandpa Jones, Minnie Pearl, Jim Reeves, Faron Young, and Patsy in New York for their Carnegie Hall performance, November 29, 1961.

**BMW 14th ANNUAL
C&W DISK JOCKEY POLL**

FAVORITE FEMALE ARTISTS OF C&W DISK JOCKEYS

Position	Artist	Label
1.	PATSY CLINE	Decca
2.	KITTY WELLS	Decca
3.	SKEETER DAVIS	RCA Victor
4.	JEAN SHEPHERD	Capitol
5.	WANDA JACKSON	Capitol
6.	ROSE MADDOX	Capitol
7.	CONNIE HALL	Mercury
8.	JAN HOWARD	Challenge
9.	SHIRLEY COLLIE	Liberty
10.	MARION WORTH	Columbia

FAVORITE MALE ARTISTS OF C&W DISK JOCKEYS

Position	Artist	Label
1.	JIM REEVES	RCA Victor
2.	MARTY ROBBINS	Columbia
3.	FARON YOUNG	Capitol
4.	BUCK OWENS	Capitol
5.	RAY PRICE	Columbia
6.	DON GIBSON	RCA Victor
7.	HANK THOMPSON	Capitol
8.	ROY DRUSKY	Decca
9. (Tie)	GEORGE JONES	Mercury
	JOHNNY CASH	Columbia

VIA AIR MAIL • CORREO AEREO

Nov 19/62

in flight — AA — **AMERICAN AIRLINES**

ROUTE OF THE ~~ASTROJETS~~ →

Dear Anne + all,

I'm headed home on an airplane after playing Worcester, Mass. last night and today at noon started to get my flight into New York from Mass, then they told us everything was grounded. So there I had to take a bus into Boston. There I get a flight for New York. In N.Y. I waited two hours and now I'm at last on my way home. I'll get in about nine o'clock and was suppose to have gotten home by two-thirty this afternoon. Oh! It's a great life. I'll get home tonite and put the kids to bed get up and pack five suit cases tomorrow all day, do a recording session tomorrow night at seven, and (pick up Mom (Charlie will) at the airport at nine, and Tues. morn-Charlie and one of the boys in the band will leave for Vegas. I'll leave with the kids and Mom (& maybe my manager) on Wed. Then start the living hell grind,

Patsy's letter to Anne Armstrong, November 19, 1962.

five

Patsy posing during the photo shoot for her album Sentimentally
Yours, *circa 1962.*

November 12, 1962

Dear Anne,

I'm headed home on an airplane after playing in Massachusetts last night. Today, at noon I started to get my flight into New York then they told us everything was grounded because of the snow so I had to take a bus into Boston. There I got a flight for New York and in New York waited for two hours. Now I'm at last on my way home.

Oh it's a great life!

I'll get home tonight and put the kids to bed and then get up and pack five suitcases tomorrow, do a recording session tomorrow night, at seven, then leave on Wednesday for Las Vegas. I thought all along that it was going to be six days a week and four shows a night working out there. Now I find, after I demanded to see the contract from Randy, that it's four shows a night, forty-five minutes each and seven days a week for five weeks. This cat's ass will be dragging the bottom out of the desert.

Oh well, that's the way the mop flops, I guess.

You should see the dresses I got for Vegas. One is a black- knit sheath, with V-neck and three-quarter sleeves with black sequins and beads covering the whole dress. The other is a knit pullover, loose up to the neck and a fitted skirt with white sequins and beads all over both pieces. And, the jewel of all, some son-of-a-bitch stole my beautiful black fox, fur trimmed collar and cuff coat. I paid $350 for it last year and there isn't another one of its kind. Stole it at the damn convention, off a coat rack, while I was just inside the door at the Decca cocktail party. Whoever it was I hope it chokes them to death before sun-up.

I put two private dicks and my Mr. Dick on it. They looked and watched all night but still no coat. I see anybody with it on I'm going to take blood, ass and all. I almost took an arm off a girl who had on one with fur trim. Charlie had to pull me off her. She was about a hundred-and-ninety pounds and almost five-foot eight. It wasn't mine. Charlie had some tall explaining to do.

I had a wonderful convention. I got Music Reporter's Star Award for 1962, Hit Award for "Crazy" and "She's Got You," and Cashbox's Favorite Female Artist 1962. I have fourteen awards all together now. I'm so proud that I could cry, and yell all at the same time. Even ol' Charlie cried when I got the "Star of the Year" award. I said, it's great to be the girl with all the awards but what the hell do I do now for '63. It's getting so Cline can't follow Cline.

Well, I'm using up all the airline's writing paper, not that I give a damn after the way my butt's been dragged around today through the snow and rain. But we're almost into Nashville.

I'll send ya pictures and cards from Vegas and y'all keep everything you've got crossed for me that I go over good out there. I still don't know that damn, crazy, act yet.

Take care and write to us. I'll send you my Vegas address as soon as I get one. Bye for now.

Love,
Patsy

H it record followed hit record for Patsy Cline in 1962. No sooner had *Crazy* reached the top than *She's Got You* began its fast climb to Number 1. Loretta Lynn recalls first hearing *She's Got You* on the radio. "I thought it was the greatest thing Patsy ever recorded. I was down in the middle of the floor waxing a hardwood floor when I heard this record. And, I said, 'Patsy's got her a smash.' When Doo, my husband, came in that night, I said, 'Patsy Cline's new record is out and it's a smash.' And, it was. I recorded it and it was Number 1 for me, too."

The song was a sentimental favorite for its author, Hank Cochran, as Billy Walker tells the story. "Hank Cochran was throwing a bash at this house and there must have been seventy-five people there. Back in those days that was one-tenth of the whole music industry in this town. He wanted to preview a new song that he had just gotten recorded and was just about to be released. It was the song *She's Got You* with Patsy. It sent chills up and down me. Boy! it was absolutely beautiful."

Hank recalls the genesis of the song. "We had been looking for songs and I didn't have anything at the time. One evening, after everybody had left, I was in my garage, which I had turned into a little studio, fumbling around by myself. I ran across a picture in a desk. I don't even remember who it was but it gave me an idea. 'I've got the picture and somebody else has got the person.' I put it all together and wrote with Patsy in mind. I called Patsy as soon as I finished and said, 'I think I've got it.' She said, 'Well go pick up a bottle and bring it over.' So I did."

Owen Bradley picks up the story from here, as he remembers how Patsy's recording of *She's Got You* moved Hank Cochran to tears. "Hank probably wouldn't like this. I remember we were back in my office and I think Hank was having a little problem at home — or something. We played back *She's Got You,* and he had tears in his eyes. He really liked Patsy's songs and we tailored several of his songs for Patsy."

She's Got You

I've got your picture
That you gave to me,
And it's signed "with love"
Just like it used to be.
The only thing diff'rent,
The only thing new,
I've got your picture,
She's got you.
I've got your memory,
Or has it got me!
I really don't know,
But I know it won't let me be.
I've got your class ring
That proved you cared,
And it still looks the same
As when you gave it, dear.
The only thing diff'rent,
The only thing new,
I've got these little things,
She's got you.

(Lyrics by Hank Cochran,
copyright 1961, Tree Publishing Co., Inc.)

**ROY
DRUSKY**

Roy Drusky remembers another occasion when Patsy's rendition of a Hank Cochran song affected him similarly. "I did write a couple of songs Patsy recorded. I'll never forget the old studio where we did a lot of recording on 16th Avenue South. Patsy had done one of my songs on this particular session. We went across the street to Decca where Owen Bradley's office was after the session. Hank Cochran, one of the great writers, had a song on the session called *Why Can't He Be You* that turned out to be a classic. I'll never forget that night — it was late, maybe midnight. When Owen played *Why Can't He Be You*, it had strings and everything on it, Hank was sitting there with tears in his eyes, just crying. He was the songwriter and that really impressed me. It's not too often that you see a writer that moved by somebody doing his song. But he was just sitting there with tears in his eyes. It was a great record. I'll always remember that. I don't remember the song of mine she did and it was on the same session."

Why Can't He Be You

He takes me to the places you and I used to go.
He tells me over and over that he loves me so.
He gives me love that I never got from you.
He loves me too, his love is true
Why can't he be you.

(Lyrics by Hank Cochran,
copyright 1962, Tree Publishing Co., Inc.)

Released in December 1961, *She's Got You*, with *Strange* on the B side, rose to Number 1 on the *Billboard* country charts and reigned for nineteen weeks, soon to be followed by the hit *So Wrong*, co-written by Carl Perkins, Mel Tillis, and Danny Dill, recorded during a major session in February 1962 as part of Patsy's third album, SENTIMENTALLY YOURS.

On 13 February 1962 Patsy was back in the Decca studio with Owen Bradley to record the songs for SENTIMENTALLY YOURS, including *So Wrong*.

So Wrong

I've been so wrong, oh yes, I was so wrong.
Why didn't I realize I was wrong?
I was so wrong, now I sing a blue, blue song.
I wasn't right, I was wrong.
Well, I never knew that I could love you, darling, oh, so much!
Now I'm in my solitude, I wait for you with your soft touch.
I've been so wrong, oh, for so long.
Darling, I wasn't right so I was wrong.

(Lyrics by Carl Perkins, Mel Tillis, and Danny Dill,
copyright 1960, 1962, Cedarwood Publishing)

Other songs recorded during that February 1993 SENTIMEN-TALLY YOURS session were several covers of hits from other eras, including *You Made Me Love You (I Didn't Want To Do It)*, first recorded by Al Jolson and then Judy Garland; *Anytime*, a song from the 1940s which became a hit for Eddy Arnold and Eddie Fisher; *Heartaches* and *That's My Desire* from the 1930s; *You Were Only Fooling (While I Was Falling In Love)*, a hit for Kay Starr; *I Can't Help It (If I'm Still In Love With You)* and *You're Cheatin' Heart* by Hank Williams; two Pee Wee King and Redd Stewart compositions, *Half As Much* and *You Belong To Me*; and *Lonely Street*, a hit for Andy Williams and Kitty Wells. In addition to the new song *So Wrong* by Perkins-Tillis-Dill, Patsy recorded *Imagine That* by Justin Tubb and *When I'm Thru With You (You'll Love Me Too)* by her songwriting standby, Harlan Howard. They also trans-formed the Hank Cochran-Jimmy Key song *You're Stronger Than Me* from Patsy's previous country version to a pop style. By June, *Imagine That* had risen to Number 20 on the charts, with *When I'm Get Thru With You* leap-frogging to Number 10.

When I'm Thru With You (You'll Love Me Too)

You think you love Sue,
But when I get thru with you,
You won't ever look at Sue again.
I'm gonna be so good to you.
I'm gonna love you my whole life thru.
Pretty soon you'll feel the same,
You won't even know her name.
I'll give you kisses that she can't beat,
I'll treat you so nice and sweet.
When I get thru with you,
You'll love me, too, not Sue;
When I get thru with you,
You'll love me, too.
I'm gonna too.

(Lyrics by Harlan Howard,
copyright 1962 by Tree Publishing Co., Inc.)

The next show-business triumph for Patsy after Carnegie Hall was playing the Hollywood Bowl on 15 June 1962, where she shared the headline with Johnny Cash for a "Shower of Stars" bill that featured country veterans Don Gibson, Mother Maybelle and the Carter Family, Leroy Van Dyke, Hank Cochran, and rising star George Jones, who remembers not so much that concert as the stunning impression Patsy made on him. "I was aware of her when she first started coming to Nashville, but, like most people, we didn't pay that much attention to anyone unless they really had their first record out and really started doing something big. When I first heard her sing, it knocked me out. We were starting to do dates on the road, working out of Nashville, with some of the people and we got to work some dates here and there with Patsy, and I just fell in love with her singing — everybody did. She was what we used to call 'a real trooper.' She'd just get right to the point and she was blunt. That's what everybody liked about her. Playing at the Hollywood Bowl was something for country music back in those days. The only thing I can remember is that Patsy did a great show — just tore the people up."

George Riddle also performed on the "Shower of Stars" tour at the Hollywood Bowl and likewise remembers her charismatic stage presence. "When Patsy hit that stage she had the audience in the palm of her hand. She took charge. She knew how to work a microphone. She knew how to talk to an audience. She didn't just get out there and sing. She'd talk to the folks and kid around with them a bit. She inspired many girl singers. You don't walk into a club, anywhere now, that you don't have a girl singer get up and do a couple of Patsy Cline songs. She took charge. Folks loved her. Patsy had charisma."

At the 11th annual WSM Country Music Festival in Nashville on 7 November 1962, Patsy Cline won an unprecedented ten awards, including the Favorite Female Artist Award from *Billboard*, the Most Programmed Album of the Year for PATSY CLINE SHOWCASE from *Cashbox*, the *Music Reporter* Female Vocalist of the Year and Star of the Year Award, and the *Music Vendor* Female Vocalist of the Year for *Crazy* and *She's Got You*.

GEORGE JONES

GEORGE RIDDLE

Patsy displaced "Country Queen" Kitty Wells as the number one female country artist for the second year in a row, and cheered as her eventual successor, Loretta Lynn, won Most Promising Female of the Year Award from *Cashbox*. To the ceremonies, she wore her now signature gold brocade suit, silver fox wrap, and fashionable spike heeled shoes.

The back-to-back-to-back success of *I Fall To Pieces*, *Crazy*, and *She's Got You* enabled Patsy's manager, Randy Hughes, to book her as the featured performer during the 1962-63 holiday season at the Meri-Mint Theater at the Mint Casino in Las Vegas, one of the first country singers, let alone a country woman, to play Vegas. The Patsy Cline show opened 23 November 1962. The Glaser Brothers, former winners, like Patsy, on *Arthur Godfrey's Talent Scouts*, were hired to back Patsy, and together they planned a show the like of which Las Vegas had never seen before, as Jim Glaser recalls. "Patsy had been contracted to work the Mint Lounge, in Las Vegas, and she was looking for a crew to do the show with her. Las Vegas could be the launching pad to bigger and better rooms in Las Vegas and bigger and better rooms around the country. Patsy was very concerned about the impression she would make out there. It was before they had remodelled the Mint Lounge and it was a surprise because it was very small — not much larger than a living room.

JIM GLASER

"Patsy put together a group of people including the band and she hired the Glaser Brothers to do some vocal backing and open the show. She wanted to do a show which, in country music, was not being done at the time. You see it more now, but then you just went out and sang your hit records. Patsy wanted to do more than that.

"She hired Gene Nash, in Nashville, to write some special material for her. Nash had been in show business all his life and his background was in dancing and record production. One day Patsy and I went over to his office, on what is now Music Row, and listened to a lot of material. She picked and chose. Some she used, some she didn't. I remember there was a version of *Mack The Knife* that Gene had written some special lyrics for. I could tell when he sang it to Patsy that she didn't like it.

"I'll never forget the spot she put me in after Nash had finished singing this country version, which was *Red The Rooster* using barnyard animals. He finished and asked Patsy what she thought. There was a pause and she turned to me and said, 'Jim, what do you think?' Put the ball right in my park.

"I said, 'I don't really think that will enhance your country image all that much.' But she did keep some of the material, especially an opening thing which was a brilliantly done piece."

CHARLIE
DICK

Charlie Dick recalls that Patsy was scared to death about appearing in Las Vegas and worried about being away from home at Christmas. "Patsy had taken the kids to her mother's to stay and was flying out from Washington. I had driven to Vegas with one of her musicians and a lot of stuff that we had to take that you didn't want to take on a plane. I got there a day early. I didn't intend to but the weather kept Patsy in Washington and she came out a day later.

"I went out that night and looked the town over to see what was happening, then the next day I went to the airport to pick her up. I think she was really scared of Vegas. She didn't want to go play the damn thing in the first place. Being away on Christmas. Christmas to Patsy and her family was very different than my family. My family, at Christmas, you got one big item — a tricycle or a wagon. Patsy's might give half a dozen gifts to the same person.

"Vegas was a big city, to what we'd been used to. I think she'd heard a lot of stories and seen a lot of movies about gambling, broads, and drinking. Plus, all the big names that were there. These were people she'd idolized all her life and she was really scared. We were downtown at the Mint. It wasn't on the Strip. She didn't know that these people didn't have shows just like you see on TV. Purposely, we didn't stop anywhere along the Strip after we picked her up. I think going in she was afraid of the schedule, seven days a week, for thirty-five days."

JIM
GLASER

Patsy didn't have any advance time to get acclimated to Las Vegas' dry climate and suffered the infamous malady, "Vegas Throat," as Jim Glaser explains. "We ultimately get to Las Vegas and neither she nor we were aware of something that happens to performers when you arrive in Las Vegas, especially when you go from a very moist climate like Nashville, Tennessee, to a very dry climate like Las Vegas, Nevada. If you don't arrive several days in advance, to give yourself time to acclimate, you get what is called Vegas Throat. This happened to Patsy. She flew in the day before the show. We had driven out and were a few days ahead so we had a chance for our voices to adjust. Come time for rehearsal on opening day, Patsy had no voice at all — could not sing a lick. She went to see the doctors that the performers went to see when they had Vegas Throat. He said the only treatment that he could give her was a very strong shot of antibiotics and not to open her mouth for three or four days. She was opening that night and the doctor told her that if she tried to sing she probably wouldn't have a voice for the entire six weeks that we were to be at the Mint Lounge.

CHARLIE DICK

"Opening night came. Everyone was there to see Patsy — a lot a people from the press and from other clubs. It was a very important thing for her. The Glaser Brothers went on and we sang our little hearts out for fifteen minutes, then they introduced Patsy."

Charlie picks up the story at this stage as he intervenes back stage. "They wouldn't give you a day off unless you were dead, so I had to go backstage and play records while she pantomimed."

Glaser continues. "She never spoke a word to the audience. She whispered. On the fourth day she came on stage and her voice was back. Her voice was so strong and powerful. She really killed them."

One of the stars in the audience was the late Carl Perkins, who caught as many of her shows as his performing schedule allowed. Patsy returned the compliment. "I used to work at the Golden Nugget quite a bit back in those years. Patsy was working directly across the street at The Mint. Boy it was hard. We used to have to do six shows a day. Forty-five minutes long — a fifteen minute break and then right back on. I had a recitation that was called 'Twenty-one.' It was about a man raising his little boy after his momma had passed away. The story evidently touched her, and every time she would come in, if I was in the middle of a song, I would cut the song short and go into 'Twenty-one' for her."

CARL PERKINS

Carl Perkins and Patsy Cline had much in common. He was a trend setter with his rockabilly music and she set musical trends that are being copied to this very day. "She set patterns that will be followed, and copied, for as long as there is good country music," Perkins explains. "If they're going to do good, they're going to have to get into the Patsy Cline way of singing because she couldn't be beat."

$$\mathscr{PC}$$

SENTIMENTALLY YOURS had been released on 6 August 1962, with an album sleeve featuring a photo of Patsy looking like a Hollywood movie matinee idol, reclining on pillows, wearing a fashionable paisley-print dress. This "high cotton" image was in keeping with her domestic life during this era when she acquired her dream home and decorated everything to her taste. As Charlie tells the story of buying the new home, "when Randy came along we needed a little bigger house. We'd always wanted a bigger house but couldn't afford it. We hadn't gone out really searching but if we saw something along the road we'd stop and look. One day Randy Hughes said his wife Kathy knew of a house on Nella Drive that we might like. We went and looked. It was almost like what Patsy had in mind — something that she wanted. It had four bed-rooms, full basement and it was almost totally complete. There was just some landscaping to be done. That just tickled her to death. The good part of it was that we didn't go out with a ton of money and say, okay, somebody go in and decorate and buy this and that. She did each room individually, picked out everything herself. I don't mean real lavish, but at least she bought what she wanted instead of having to take what she could afford."

Her Hillhurst Drive neighbor Joyce Blair regretted losing her next-door status with Patsy but remained a dear friend. "She came over and told us that she had bought this house. I was very sad. I hated to lose her as my good friend and neighbor. She wanted me to see the new house. I understood why she wanted this big, beautiful home. She could afford it now. The home was beautiful, and I was really happy for her. It wasn't too long that she got to enjoy her home. But she loved it so much, she couldn't wait to get home."

Patsy paid special attention to decorating the bedrooms for Julie and Randy, as Charlie recalls. "Julie's beautiful canopy bed was something that all little girls want when they are little. I think Patsy probably wanted one herself and never had one. Little boys should have bunk beds so Randy got them. She put a magnolia tree we got from a florist in our living room. It was in a big bucket. She said that house in the neighborhood always had a lamp sitting in the picture window — she didn't want one. I thought that was a little weird at first, but it turned out pretty good.

"Patsy ordered a sofa for the living room. She'd found some material she wanted but couldn't find a sofa with that material so had it made. It was wait, wait, wait and finally they called and said the sofa was ready. Patsy was called to the phone when they brought it in. I told them to just leave it there and we'd arrange it. She came into the living room and gasped. She was about to take the picture window out because they put the arm on the wrong piece of furniture. It was sectional and the arm was on the wrong piece.

"That house was her baby. The only thing I had anything to do with was the den. I helped decorate the den and the bar. She probably had these things on her mind for a hundred years, and just knew what she wanted and was just waiting to get the money to do it. It was really special."

Her daughter Julie has especially fond memories of the new house, even though she was only four years old at the time. "I remember a lot about that house. When I first looked for a house for myself, I watched to see if it ever came up for sale. I remember the layout completely, the way it was decorated and everything. The day that I got my furniture, I ran up the sidewalk, fell, and skinned my knee. My grandmother and mother were there. One of them happened to have some antiseptic in her purse and painted my knee. I went running to the bedroom — the new white canopy, the desk with the chair with material on the seat. I climbed on the chair and left an orange mark on it. The bed is still in the family and, as far as I know, that mark is still on that chair.

"Every piece of furniture fit the house. There was a mural on

JOYCE
BLAIR

CHARLIE
DICK

JULIE
FUDGE

105

the wall in the dining room. My grandmother said it was an apple orchard, which would make you think of Virginia where she was from. I remember shopping with her. I remember the stores that we went in. I'm not sure Daddy can recall better. I remember a lot of those things. I don't feel like anybody has ever told me those things — ever. Those things, I just remember."

Patsy's friend Margie Beaver paints a picture of Patsy as a content homemaker in her new house, the epitome of maternal and domestic bliss. "She loved home life. I can remember her enjoying being in the kitchen — no makeup on, hair not particularly fancy or flashy, cotton dress. That was the homemaker side of her. Even though she was pursuing a career, she was able to put those things behind her and become a homemaker."

Despite the spoils of fame, Patsy remained a sentimental yet joyful parent, as she let Anne Armstrong know in a letter.

1962

Dear Anne,

The kids are fine and mean as hell. Randy got his first black eye. They were fighting over a coat hanger, and Julie let it go and it popped him in the eye. Busted a blood vessel but he's okay now.

Charlie's tried to be with me on the road, but I hate to leave the kids without one of us too long. We'll try to work something out, but my time is going to be limited from the way my manager rattled off my bookings last night. Have just enough time to change my drawers between bookings.

Well, I'll close now.

Love,
Patsy

As Charlie Dick explains, Patsy was a loving, caring mother, and worried constantly about the children when she was on the road. "Patsy always worried about the children whenever she was on the road. She knew that Sophie was a good a baby sitter and ninety-percent of the time I was within phone contact. She'd call home, even when she couldn't afford it. She'd call at least every day, sometimes she'd call two or three times a day. She'd be lonesome and use the kids for an excuse to call home. She was very worried about the kids because she was gone so much. There was no reason in particular she should have been except just a mother's love and being far away from home."

Loretta Lynn also has bitter-sweet memories of the dream home on Nella Drive, which she visited only two months before Patsy died. When Patsy invited Loretta to see her new home, she remembers how happy and proud she was. "When Patsy bought her house — it was a little brick house — she was so proud of it. She got her furniture and everything and says, 'Come out here, Loretta.' So I went out with her and she says, 'Look at this. Isn't it pretty?' I said, 'It sure is, Patsy.' She says, 'Now I won't be happy 'till I have bought my momma one, just like it.' Patsy lived about two months after that."

CHARLIE DICK

LORETTA LYNN

107

Patsy in her "high cotton" days.

Patsy standing outside and performing inside the Merri-Mint Theatre, Las Vegas, Christmas, 1962.

Patsy's dream home at 815 Nella Drive, Goodlettsville, 1962–63.

Patsy at home on Nella Drive.

Patsy with the boys: (left to right) Gordon Terry, Luther Perkins, Carl Perkins, and George Jones, 1962.

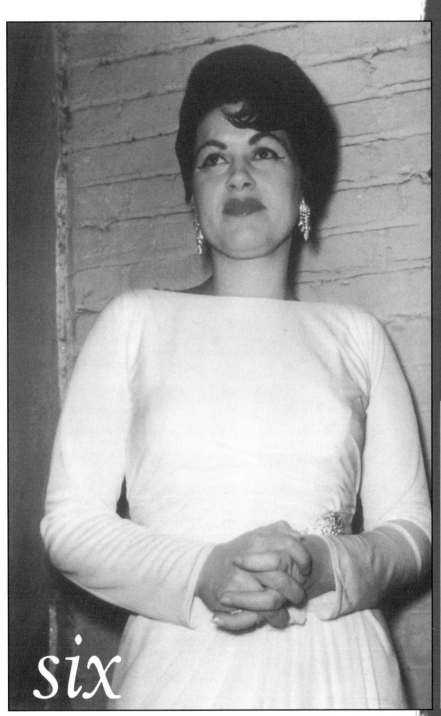

six

Patsy backstage before her final concert.

February 10, 1963

Dear Anne:

Well, I just finished a new album. They say this one is going to be the best one yet, number one. I sure hope so. I know I worked my fanny off on it.

We sure put some crazy beats on some of the old songs. We put "Blue Moon of Kentucky" with a bosa nova beat to it and did "Crazy Arms" with a Mexican beat. The other songs we put in are "Faded Love," "Sweet Dreams," "Always," "Does Your Heart Beat for Me," "Bill Bailey," "Love Letters in the Sand," "He Called Me Baby All Night Long," "I'll Sail My Ship Alone" and "Someday." It will be the last of March when it comes out, they say.

The big bad John, Jimmy Dean, dropped by my session the other night and said, 'I see you're still singing your ass off,' and I said to him, 'I see you're still as big headed as you Texans always are.'

I don't know when we'll be up that way again and it don't look like I'm going to get any time off from next week-end on. I go to Trenton, New Jersey, this coming weekend and the next week to North Carolina and then down to Birmingham, Alabama. In between I've got to record again. So you can see I won't have much time to goof off.

Well, I must close now and get busy with supper. We're all well and hope all that way are the same.

Take care and write.

Love to all,
Patsy

By 1963, Patsy's life as a recording artist and concert performer had taken on a yearly pattern: record a new album of songs in February, tour from late spring to early fall, then pick up her awards in November during the WSM Country Music Festival. The February 1993 recording session produced some of her greatest songs, notably the Bob Wills classic, *Faded Love,* and the Don Gibson classic, *Sweet Dreams.* The session was again produced by Owen Bradley, with her regular session musicians, Floyd Cramer on piano, Harold Bradley on bass guitar, Grady Martin on lead guitar, Randy Hughes on acoustic guitar, and the Jordanaires on backing vocals. The lyrics, the music, the musicians, the producer, and the singer were a recipe for success once again. However, the February 1963 session would be the last session for the singer.

Owen Bradley recalls this last session with Patsy. "By now we were sort of into a little pattern and we were using strings on most of the songs, a lot of the songs. We were making an album, and we approached an album a little different than we did a single. The singles were a little more country and we had songs in there that on an album we wouldn't necessarily go for a single, *Sweet Dreams* being one of them. It had already been out by Don Gibson and some others. Anyway it was a big hit by more than one artist, so we were just making it as an album song. We had some other songs at that time that were standards, and this really was like a blessing because it gave us some songs that have lasted and I think it probably kept her music alive a lot longer because some of the songs were maybe not that good. The good ones have stayed.

"We did *Faded Love,* which was one of Patsy's favorites. That would probably be the most outstanding thing that we did in that last session because she wanted to sing it all in the same key — and it was difficult to sing in one key. Originally, it was written in two keys to take care of the range. She insisted on singing it in the same key and really did, really put a brand on it, too. I think everybody in the session really enjoyed making that record. I know she really loved it. She had invited Dottie West and Jan Howard, Harlan and Hank up to my office, after the session and we played

OWEN BRADLEY

the album back. Patsy was very proud of it. That's really the last time that I saw her, and she seemed very pleased with all of her cuts. It was on a happy note that we ended that last session."

Charlie Dick tells the story behind Patsy's desire to record *Faded Love* in one key or octave. "One time we were coming back from Virginia and Patsy was in the back seat. I thought she was asleep. I had the radio on and Jackie Deshannon came on. She had just recorded *Faded Love*. There's a modulation in it. The range is so great that they modulate to get it all in. Jackie Deshannon modulated just like Bob Wills.

CHARLIE DICK

"Patsy comes up from the back seat and says, 'Why did she modulate?' I said that everybody I know modulates.

"Patsy said, 'They probably have to because they can't do it all in the same octave. Well, I can.'

"I was tired driving and said, 'Big deal.'

"The next time she saw Owen she said, 'Sometime I want to cut *Faded Love* and I'm not going to modulate.'"

Jan Howard was in the studio when Patsy recorded *Faded Love*. She shocked Jan when she kidded about it being her last record. "I remember being at the session when she recorded *Faded Love*," Jan recalls. "It was a very special time for me because I was such a fan and by that time had become a friend. I had a thing about going to other people's sessions. I never did if I wasn't invited to go. I felt it was business, and I know when I was recording a lot, there would be people in the studio that I didn't want there and that distracted me. Now friends were a different story.

JAN HOWARD

"Patsy called me that afternoon and said, 'Are you coming down to the session?' I said, 'Well no, I hadn't planned to,'" and she said, 'Well why don't you come down. I'd like you to be there.' I said, 'Okay, I'll be there.' That was a compliment to me that she wanted me to come. There were a bunch of people there. I remember Dottie West.

"Patsy sang *Faded Love* with the Jordanaires. I can't remember what other songs were on that session, that one just stuck in my mind. When the session was over, she laughed, that big laugh of hers, and told the Jordanaires to come back tomorrow night. She was so happy, so up. We went up to Owen's office and listened to the recording. A thing that I remember so well, and it really gives me cold chills to this day, she went into Harry Silverstein's office (Owen's assistant) and was in there for a while. She came back with a record. It was her first record, *A Church, A Courtroom And Then Goodbye.*

"She said, 'Well here it is, the first and the last.'

"I said, 'God! Don't say that.'

"Patsy said, 'Oh,I just meant the first recording and this one, don't get so upset.' It really got to me, especially later."

Many other country artists, like her friend Dottie West, consider *Faded Love* to be Patsy's best song and point out the sobbing catch in her voice on the closing bars as proof positive that she really felt what she was singing. Dottie watch Patsy record both *Faded Love* and *Sweet Dreams* — and witnessed the emotional impact both songs had on her. "I watched her do both of them in the studio and there were tears literally streaming down her face because she just put her heart, and soul, into the music."

Faded Love

As I look at the letters you wrote to me,
It's you that I'm thinking of.
As I read the lines that to me were so sweet,
I remember our faded love.
I miss you, darling, more and more every day
As heaven would miss the stars above.
With every heart beat I still think of you,
And remember our faded love.

(Lyrics by John Wills and Bob Wills, copyright 1950, 1951
by Bob Wills Music, Inc. and Unichapppell Music Inc. (Rightsong Music).

For guitarist Don Helms, *Sweet Dreams* from this session was as great as *I Fall To Pieces.* In the studio, Patsy had the same presence as Hank Williams, with whom Helms had worked previously. "Back then everybody made a record together — the singer and all the musicians were there at one time. It's a little different today. They lay the sound track down with the musicians and then they go to another session and the singer comes in. Patsy would work right with the musicians. We didn't have the number system like they have today. Somebody would play a little bit of a demo or the singer would sing a few lines. Everybody kind of learned the song and then we'd just go from there. You'd just create something that would fit what you're doing at the time.

"Owen had the complete respect of the musicians and singers. He could get the job done with the musicians he had. When I was working with Hank Williams, it seemed like everybody would just stand back and watch Hank Williams with awe. They did the same thing with Patsy Cline. When she sang, all the other girl singers would gather around and watch her. I would say that she and Hank had a lot in common. They had complete confidence in what they were doing. They could get the audience right in the palm of their hands."

PC

CHARLIE DICK

Patsy Cline's drive to succeed, on her own terms, was infamous, as was the colorful language she laid on those who deliberately or accidentally tried to way-lay her. Charlie Dick offers an anecdote about this trait in her character. "It all goes back to the beginning like the Godfrey thing. She wanted it so bad. They accepted her but didn't accept the group. She wouldn't stay. But she wouldn't give up. She went back and tried again. She wanted the Opry bad and back then you had to have a hit song to get on. It was pretty cliquey in Nashville. But she didn't give a damn, she was going to go after it anyway.

"Then in Atlanta one night, I think it was around Thanksgiving, there were three or four people on the show, and when it came her turn to go over her songs with the band they asked her what she was going to sing. Patsy says one of her songs was *White Christmas*. Faron Young, one of the other stars on the show, came over and said it was too early to sing *White Christmas*. The only reason he said it was too early was because he hadn't thought of it first. Patsy started rehearsing and he kept on bugging in the background that it was too early. Patsy reached over and shook the hell out of him and said, 'I'll sing anything I want to until it's your show, so shut your mouth!' And she did."

Patsy "was the type of person that could handle herself," her friend Margie Beaver explains, "because of her personality, because of all the many sides of her. If she had to stand her ground and say something, she didn't hesitate. She could chew you out. If you knew her very well, you were not surprised to have her curse you a little bit or cuss you out." While another friend, Joyce Blair, never heard Patsy swear in her company, she recognized her drive and determination. "Patsy never cussed in front of us, never. Now maybe it was because, with us, she was more at ease. But she had to be aggressive. She once said, 'You have to get in there and punch to get any place.'" As Del Wood explains, a little profanity goes with the territory. "If she used all those four-letter words, she didn't use them around me. I don't think she did, except when she was angry, and who doesn't."

Following her February recording sessions, Patsy was invited by Harry "Hap" Peebles, the largest promoter in the Midwest, to perform at a benefit concert for "Cactus Jack" Call in Kansas City on 3 March 1963. Call, the most popular country music deejay in the area, had died in January as a result of an automobile accident and left his wife and children with little money. Peebles looked to Hawkshaw Hawkins and Billy Walker for assistance in lining up performers for a benefit, and Walker in turn approached Patsy's manager, Randy Hughes. The bill soon included Patsy, Randy's father-in-law Cowboy Copas, Roy Acuff, George Jones, Dottie West, Grand Ole Opry announcer Ralph Emery, the Clinch Mountain Clan, Hawkshaw Hawkins, and Billy Walker.

As Walker recalls, Randy Hughes agreed to let Patsy perform for free at the "Cactus" Jack Call benefit show and made plans to fly her to Kansas City in his own plane, along with Walker, Hawkins, and Copas. "Randy Hughes was a soft spoken type of a guy. He had a lot of common sense when it came to promoting artists. There's a lot of people that don't even realize that it was Randy on guitar behind Patsy and behind me on the Opry. He had a good home life. Kathy, his wife, was really a beautiful lady. Randy had a sixth sense about people becoming stars.

MARGIE BEAVER

JOYCE BLAIR

DEL WOOD

BILLY WALKER

"I came to Randy and said, 'Randy, we're trying to put this show together, and he said, 'Okay, you can count on me.' I asked if he thought Patsy would do it, and he said he was sure she would because Patsy was the type of person that would help anybody who was down. She proved it. So we not only got Patsy but Cowboy Copas, who was Randy's father-in-law. He said he would go. I talked to Hawkshaw Hawkins and Guy Smith, who was helping me with the arrangements. Guy had talked to Roy Acuff and then George Jones and made a deal with them to come by. Dottie West was on her way through and decided that she would come in. We ended up with a gigantic list of performers for this show."

The plan was for Randy Hughes to pick up Billy Walker at the Nashville airport and fly him to Kansas City, along with Patsy, but fate intervened, as it did on the return flight, Walker explains. "I had made arrangements with Randy before he went to Montgomery to come back to Nashville and pick me up here at the airport to go to Kansas City. Instead, I had to go early and fly on to Kansas City before they got back into town. That's why I didn't go to Kansas City with them."

Neither did Charlie Dick, who chose to stay in Nashville to take care of Julie and young Randy when the two other passengers, Cowboy Copas and Hawkshaw Hawkins, came on board the four-seat airplane. "Patsy had a booking on Saturday in Birmingham. We went to Birmingham, Randy, Patsy, and myself. The first show was sold out before the doors were opened. The second show was sold out immediately after the first show started. After the second show had started there were still five hundred people standing outside wanting to see the show and there was no show. Randy asked me if Patsy would do a third show. I say, 'Yeah!' They did the third, a very short one. It was one of her biggest dates.

"Patsy, Randy, and I arrived back into Nashville from Birmingham around eight or eight-thirty Sunday morning the 3rd of March. Sometime, during the previous week, Hawkshaw and Copas had decided that they would go to Kansas City. It was only a four-seater plane, so I said there is no reason for me to go. It's a free show and you all go in one plane and save the fare. Plus, the kids were here and I could take care of them for the rest of the weekend. While we were unloading and loading I said something about I'm glad y'all are getting out of town. Now I've got the night free and I can go out and do whatever I want to. Patsy said, if I did, she may perform a little operation on me when she got home. I said I might even go by Copas's house, and Cop said, 'Well I hope you have a little better luck than I do.' Everybody was in a jolly, joking, mood when they left. The weather was good, they had no fear of going then, nothing about flying a little plane or anything like that. It was just fun time."

During the late 1950s and early 1960s, country and pop music performers began to travel from concert venue to venue on small chartered planes because it was faster and far more comfortable than having five people, plus a bass fiddle, in a Coupe de Ville, as Roy Drusky explains. "That's the way you traveled back in those days. There were no interstates, there were two lane roads. It's crowded, you know. Of course, we were looking for better ways of transportation. Suddenly we discovered that an airplane was the best way to get from point A to point B. We started flying because there had to be an easier way. I had a plane and, matter of fact, I flew Randy Hughes over to St. Louis to pick up the plane that Patsy and them were in. I've never forgotten the plane's number — 7000P. I said, 'Man Randy, that's a lucky number on that plane.' All these years that really stuck with me because I though that's a great number — 7000P."

The flight from Nashville to Kansas City was uneventful and Billy Walker was waiting at the airport for the plane to land. "I met Randy at the airport with a limousine and got them down to the auditorium. We did two shows that night."

As Harry "Hap" Peebles recalls those two shows, "I was to M.C. the show. Patsy was in great shape for that particular show. She was the life of the party. At the time *Crazy* and *Walkin' After Midnight* and some of her other big songs were on the charts. She was probably one of the top two girl singers in the nation." As does George Jones. "I remember us working together. I just fell in love with her singing, like everybody did. We were all kind of built up, real high, in our heads that night. As usual she did a great show,

RAY
DRUSKY

BILLY
WALKER

121

just tore the people up. I remember coming into the dressing room with Cowboy Copas. His daughter had fixed him a whole chicken — fried it for him to take in this little oblong container you could see through. He'd say, 'George, won't you have a piece of chicken, my daughter Kathy fixed for me before I left home.' I said, 'No, I'm not hungry right now. I can't sing on a full stomach.' But, eventually, I came back in there and ate every piece of chicken that was in the container. I've thought of that many times. I'm sure he didn't mind."

Dottie West shared a dressing room with Patsy at the auditorium and remembers the foreboding weather that night as Patsy, Randy, Cowboy Copas, and Hawkshaw Hawkins planned their return flight to Nashville. "There was bad weather and it rained on the day we were doing the show. But there was still a big crowd and we did two shows, an afternoon matinee and an evening show. I shared a dressing room with Patsy and we had such a great time. We laughed and talked. I don't remember the exact conversation but it was always fun to be with her. She wore the most gorgeous, white chiffon, dress. She did close the show, because she was the star.

"I watched both shows and I will never forget that white chiffon dress. I thought, my God she sings like an angel and she looks like one. She was just beautiful. She sang so effortlessly — it was so easy. They just screamed and yelled when she did *Bill Bailey, Won't You Please Come Home?* She was really happy that day and evening.

"Later, we had a sandwich together, and then everybody said goodnight. The next morning we had breakfast together in the hotel restaurant. Hawkshaw Hawkins joined us. There was a big, round table. Cowboy Copas sat at a table alone. Now that I look back I see that big white hat sitting there at the table alone. I guess he got done a little earlier. Maybe he was reading the paper, whatever. Patsy picked up the check. She just loved to do those kind of things and it was from the heart. She almost rode back to Nashville in the car with Bill and me, rather than flying, because Randy kept going to the phone and calling the weather bureau. There were no flights — it was a bad, foggy rain. The last thing I said to Patsy was I'm really going to be worried about you flying in this weather. She said, 'Don't worry about me hoss! When it's my time to go it's my time.' Hoss was an affectionate little word that she used. That was the last thing she said."

Harry "Hap" Peebles recalls walking out of the hotel that Monday morning with Patsy. "We all stayed at what was then the Townhouse Motor Hotel, in Kansas City, and what was later the Ramada Inn, just a couple of blocks from Memorial Hall where we had played the Call benefit. The following morning, it was raining, and Patsy and I walked out of the building together. She was going to the airport and I was going back to Wichita." The weather proved to be too unsettled for Randy to get clearance to fly his single-engine four-seater Commanche, so they stayed over another night in Kansas City, Charlie Dick explains. "I talked to Patsy on Monday. She said they weren't coming home until Tuesday. Our Randy was a little bit sick. He had a cold."

Although Billy Walker had planned to take Hawkshaw Hawkins' place on the return flight to Nashville while Hawkshaw traveled back by a commercial airliner, they traded places, Billy recalls. "That night we didn't get through until about midnight and then we had a press party at the hotel. It lasted about an hour. I had to settle up because I paid everybody's transportation. I settled with Randy for the use of his plane and said goodnight to Patsy. It must have been around one in the morning.

"I had gotten a call earlier that evening from my wife. Her father had a heart attack and I had to get back to Nashville as quick as possible. I was on the hotel elevator with Hawkshaw Hawkins and I said, 'Hawk I'm in a dilemma. I've got to get back to Nashville as quick as I can.' He pulled out this open airline ticket, that I had given him earlier, and said, 'Here kid.' He was about two inches taller than I was. He said, 'I'll fly back with Randy and them. I flew over with them and I trust him.' They couldn't fly out Monday and flew out sometime Tuesday."

Because the weather had not cleared on Tuesday, Walker was concerned about the safety of Randy and his passengers, calling Randy's wife Kathy at home in Nashville several times that day for any information she may have heard about the flight. "I had gotten back to Nashville and my wife had gone to Texas to be at her father's bedside. He was dying. All day Tuesday I became very worried and I called Randy's house, three or four times to see about him. I called about seven o'clock. Kathy said, 'I just hung up the phone from Randy. He's in Dyersburg.' I said, 'Thank God. I have been extremely concerned all day about them getting home.' That's the last time anybody heard from them."

BILL BRAESE

Randy Hughes had flown the plane from Kansas City to Dyersburg, Tennessee, about 150 miles from Nashville, without any real problems. Airport manager Bill Braese recalls Randy calling his wife and still remains puzzled why Randy reported that the sun was shining in Nashville while a storm was brewing in Dyersburg. "When I heard that Randy had called his wife and that the sun was shining in Nashville, I realized that couldn't be. I took Randy down the hallway and outside between the airport building and flight service station. I pointed the bank of clouds out to him, which at this time was highlighted by the setting sun and very, very, plain. You could see it very well. He decided that he would go as far as he could and come back if he couldn't get in."

EVELYN BRAESE

Evelyn Braese, co-manager of the airport, describes the weather that evening. "The closest weather reporting, at that time, would have been from Jackson, Tennessee, which would be twenty-five miles southwest of Camden. The weather that was going through in the Jackson area was showing the bases of clouds around 1,300 feet. Visibility was running about five miles in light, occasionally moderate rain and some fog mixed in with it. The weather that came through about and hour-and-a-half before they landed in Dyersburg was heavy, heavy rain. We had some winds that had even broken the tie-down on one of our airplanes. The airplane bounced around in the wind and damaged the wing tip of another airplane."

Leroy Neil, who worked at the Dyersburg Airport, gave Randy a weather briefing. "My job was to brief the pilots. The weather was what we described as visual flight rules. The weather was worse to the east of us towards Nashville. As I recall the events, the pilot came into the weather station and his passengers came over to the restaurant. I didn't know who the passengers were until the next day. It was a routine brief. It was March weather — thunderstorms, spring weather. It wasn't part of our jobs to advise whether to go or not. We treated them as professionals. We gave them the weather and then they made up their own minds. We didn't have any authority to tell the pilot whether he should go or not. The pilot was well mannered, as I recall, easy to talk to and easy to communicate with. I don't recall that he seemed tired or exhausted. At that time radar information was, you might say, non-existent. Now we have radar maps. At that time you had to rely on the teletype description as far as Dyersburg and Nashville were concerned. You didn't have any radar to look at. You had your forecast. It would say, thunderstorms, a front in a certain position, thunderstorms, lightning."

NEIL LEROY

Significantly, Randy Hughes was not trained to fly by instrument and had little training or experience flying in extreme weather conditions, as his friend Harlan Howard adds. "Randy Hughes had a licence to follow a highway from here to there. He wasn't an instrument pilot and highly trained."

HARLAN HOWARD

While Leroy Neil deferred to Randy's professional judgment, Bill Braese realized the weather would be a serious problem and did his best to warn Randy of the danger. "I explained to Randy that fronts will stall over a body of water. A front will go across at say, 30 mph but, when it hits the lake, it may drop down to 10 mph." As Evelyn Braese adds, "The squall line carries imbedded thunderstorms and within the thunderstorms can be very violent weather. A mile away on the fringes of the thunderstorm it might be moderate rain and wind. But, in the center of the thunderstorm it can be tremendous — turbulence, hail, heavy rain. It could destroy an airplane in the air."

In spite of these warnings, Randy decided to take off for Nashville. Bill and Evelyn Braese told him they would wait in case he decided to turn back, Bill explains. "He decided that he would go as far as he could and come back if he couldn't get in. I told him where the nearest airport to the lake was. I said, 'If you can't see the airport, turn around and come back. We'll wait until you come back.' We waited until ten o'clock or so, until I figured he's either on the ground or ran out of gas.

BILL BRAESE

"He was supposed to call when he got there, which he didn't do, so we closed up the restaurant and went to the house. His last words were that if he couldn't make it he'd turn around and come back."

We know nothing more about the flight from Dyersburg to Nashville other than the plane crashed near Camden, Tennessee, with all aboard dying. Charlie Dick heard from two friends that a plane was missing and suspected it was Randy's. "Billy Graves (Nashville producer) and Hubert Long heard through the grapevine that the plane was missing so they came to the house and spent the biggest part of the night." Charlie Dick recalls telling his daughter that her mother was dead. "I went into Julie's bedroom and laid down on the bed with her and told her about it. I don't think it really soaked in at the time. When she saw all the people I think it got to her."

As Julie recalls, "I was four-and-a-half. There's a lot things I don't remember because I was small. But I remember a lot more than I thought I would. Daddy woke me up and told me and there were a lot of people around. The Carters (June and "Mother" Maybelle) were there and I remember I didn't feel well. I believe it was 'Momma' that took care of me. She laid me down in Momma and Daddy's room. We had a dog, a little poodle, and I remember the lady across the street took me and the dog to the vet to kind of get me out, or do something different, with all the commotion going on."

The morning of 6 March 1963 *The Nashville Banner* ran the headline, "4 Opry Stars Die in Crash," with a front-page photograph of police officers and funeral home attendants combing through the wreckage, as well as photos of the deceased. The plane had crashed during extremely turbulent weather in a heavily wooded area of rugged hills about a mile off Highway 70, three miles west of Camden. Ken Leggitt, a licensed pilot who was studying at the time for exams, visited the crash site early on the morning of March 6. "On the night of March 5th I was studying for exams. It was pouring rain, lightning, maybe thunder — real bad March night. The next morning I got up at four o'clock and the Chicago radio station I listened to said that the plane carrying Patsy Cline had been lost and they were searching for it somewhere near Camden, Tennessee. I was a good friend with the Chief of Police in nearby Paris, Tennessee, so I drove to the police station. They were listening to the radios of the searchers. They said that they thought they had spotted it, and the Chief said he was going. I went with him. They had just found them. It was in a ravine along the railroad, in a heavy wooded area.

"The plane had gone in at a very step angle. You could see the trees were cut, you could see the exact angle. It impacted at a very high speed. The nose was down, about thirty degrees and the back about twenty degrees. The engine block was the only recognizable thing, and it was covered with mud and water. They had to pump water out of there to get to what was left of the bodies, except those that were strung in the trees and the pieces of the airplane. There were a few things around recognizable — a big cowboy hat, hairspray, personal effects. Primarily, it was nothing but pieces of wreckage, strewn over the whole area. It was really a bad scene."

Ken Leggitt also reconstructed the cause of the crash and course of the flight from Dyersburg. "Their intended route was approximately 150 miles (from Dyersburg to Nashville). They would have been flying approximately 30 minutes and covered about 65 to 70 miles (by the time they reached the Camden area), at which point they would have lost the V.O.R. (Visual Omnigator Radio) navigational system at Dyersburg because they were so low, and they were too far from Nashville to pick it up on the other side. That's probably where they had the first problem. He (Randy) had no signal. He had nothing but his compass to go by, so he was keeping below the clouds. I believe the report was that he was at six or seven hundred feet, or less, and the terrain rises there where he crashed. He couldn't go into the clouds. You can't fly a plane on instruments unless you've been trained to fly one on instruments.

"There was a tremendous amount of damage done by the impact, including the complete shearing of the prop, which was done in the hole.

"Later I saw the accident report and it and it confirmed what

I had figured. I had my commercial licence back at the time, and I knew then that a pilot that was not authorized to fly instruments had flown into an area where there were instruments required. He just couldn't handle the airplane and flew it into the ground. That's just what happened."

For Harlan Howard, the parallels between the fatal crashes killing Patsy Cline and Jim Reeves within the same year were tragic in the hubris shown by the pilots. Like Randy Hughes, Jim Reeves was not trained as an instrument pilot, and like Randy, didn't have the training or experience for flying through turbulent skies. "It became the thing to send the band by car — let them drive down those blue highways — and you fly there — zip in and zip out. Except some of these people weren't all that highly qualified to fly these planes, like Randy Hughes. He wasn't an instrument pilot and highly trained. The same thing happened to Jim Reeves. Too much self-confidence. There was a storm over Brentwood — he just flew right through it. There must of been a whirl wind or tornado and boom! We lost him and I was in a state of shock because we'd lost what I consider our top male singer and our top female singer. They were my friends and I loved them — just in a year and the same doggone way. After that there was a whole bunch of planes went up for sale."

Roger Miller and Billy Graves asked if Charlie Dick wanted to go with them to the crash scene. "Billy Graves and Roger Miller wanted to know if I wanted to go with them, and I said no, I'd better stay here because I've got the kids. At the time we didn't know what was at the crash scene or who it was. So I stayed. As I recall one of them (Julie or Randy) woke up and I went in and laid across the bed to keep them quiet. That's when I half dozed. Billy Walker came into the room. I realized somebody was in the room. I heard on the radio that they found the plane and there were no survivors."

Graves and Miller were not the only country stars and friends of Patsy to visit the scene. Carl Perkins changed his plans for the day when he heard about the crash early that morning. "I was going fishing, it was about five o'clock in the morning. I heard a local disc jockey. He was talking about it. I lived in Jackson,

HARLAN
HOWARD

CHARLIE
DICK

Tennessee (approximately 50 miles from Camden) I just unhooked from my fishing boat and took off. The roads were barricaded and the Highway Patrol wouldn't let you in. I had a State (priority) licence plate, and when they saw I had a 150 number they let me go back to the crash site.

"I picked up a compact that said, 'Made Especially for Patsy Cline' on the outside, a tube of lipstick, and a hair brush. They're in the Country Hall of Fame."

CARL PERKINS

Many of Patsy's friends and colleagues later recalled conversations with her days before her death which seemed to foreshadow the events. Others remember how close they came to dying with her. Patsy had told Jan Howard that all she wanted to do the weekend of the Cactus Jack Call benefit was get home from Kansas City because she and Charlie were leaving immediately on a flying vacation with Randy Hughes and his wife. Jan hoped it wasn't going to be in Randy's one-engine plane. "Just before she went to Kansas City, we were in the beauty salon and she was tired. She said, 'I'm dreading going up there,' but she had to. She said when they got back from that, she, Charlie, Randy, and Kathy were going to go to the Bahamas on a vacation. I said, 'Not in that little one engine thing, I hope.'

"She said, 'Yeah! we'll go over there.'

"I said, 'I wish wouldn't fly in that thing. There's one engine and if it goes out what happens — you go down.'

"She said, 'Well, if the little bug goes down, I guess we'll go down with it.' I remember that clearly. That is not a good memory."

Jan also tells the story of an occult experience the night of Patsy's death she shared with Hank Cochran. "The night Patsy was killed, the night the plane went down, I was asleep. Hank Cochran called me and he said, 'Are you alright?'

JAN HOWARD

"It was one o'clock in the morning, and I said, 'Yeah!'

"He said, 'Well I'm in Fred Foster's office and two albums have just fallen off his office shelves, mine and Patsy's.' He said he knew something had happened to one of us.

"I said, 'I'm alright.'

"And he said, 'Then it's Patsy.'"

Ferlin Husky, Patsy's management 'stable-mate' under Randy Hughes, was woken during the middle of the night to be told about the crash. He was so shaken that he couldn't perform that evening. "I was working in Coco Beach. There was a night club there. Lightnin' Chance was with me. Lightnin' was real close with Randy for years — he played bass. He woke me up and told me. I couldn't believe it. It's still hard to believe but I remember exactly what I was doing. I didn't work that night. I couldn't work that night."

Mel Tillis filled in for Ferlin Husky that night. "I was down at Cape Canaveral at the time. I was with a buddy of mine. We went to see, and hear, Ferlin Husky perform at a big club for the space people. Then we heard the news (about the plane crash) and it just about killed Ferlin. Not only did Ferlin have his manager (Randy Hughes) flying the plane, he was also Patsy's manager. I can't even describe how it felt. It was just horrible. It was just hard even to think about. I recall that he couldn't perform so I went in and I filled in for him that night. I can't even describe how it felt — it was just horrible. Randy was always pretty careless. I'm not putting the blame on him but he used to get in a car and drive 110 mph, just as fast as he could. I loved Randy, he was just a go-getter — the weather got him."

Ray Walker of the Jordanairs remembers Patsy's back-stage farewell after her last performance at the Grand Ole Opry. "We were standing at the back of the Ryman and, as I remember it, there were two or three of us standing there. She hugged us and I can see her walking towards those steps going out back of the Ryman stage. 'Patsy, be careful,' I said.

She turned, flipped the collar of her fur coat, looked back with those flashing eyes. 'Honey! I've had two bad wrecks already. The third one will either be a charm or it will kill me.'"

The week before the crash on Thursday, Patsy and Charlie had surprised Loretta Lynn with a special gift; at the same time, Patsy invited Loretta to travel with her to Kansas City to perform at the benefit. "Patsy bought my curtains and sneaked them over to my house while I was in town. She and Charlie hung the curtains, then they called the office that was trying to book me, at the time, and told me to come home. Patsy wanted to talk to me about going with her on a trip. That was Thursday, before she was killed. She hung my drapes. When I got home I looked around, and my goodness, they were orange. I had a glass sliding door — they stood out. I've still got my curtains. She asked me to go with her (to Kansas City). She told me she would give me fifty dollars. Fifty dollars was like a million dollars to me. Now that was Thursday and I said, 'Okay, I'll go.' On Friday I called her and told her that I had a job making seventy-five dollars and I was going to stay. I would have been on that trip with her."

Patsy's good friend, Annie Armstrong, still can't talk about Patsy's death without her eyes brimming with tears. "We heard it on the morning news. We listened to the Grand Ole Opry. It was awful sad. I can't even talk about it. I'll probably start crying. We called Charlie. I think he was taking it better than we were. Patsy had a lot of fans in Guelph. We all had Patsy Cline records and we would have a Patsy Cline party. It was a sad day."

Joyce Blair recalls the conversation she had with Patsy in the beauty shop a few weeks before her death and the promise Patsy made her make to care for her children should she die. "We went to the same beauty shop together, and two weeks before her accident Patsy came in just bubbling as always and said, 'Blair, I want to talk to you.' We sat and talked for quite some time and she said, 'If anything ever happens to me will you go to my babies?'

"'Patsy, what are you talking about?'

"'I just want you to know that I love you and Big Daddy and I just feel that you would do anything I asked you to do.'

"I said, 'Sure Patsy we'd be more than happy to do anything. But honey, nothing's going to happen to you.'

"'Well, I just want to make sure. I've got my kids taken care of for the rest of their lives. I think sometime I'm going to come off the road. I'm so tired of traveling all the time. I've always told you that I want to go to church, have my family, and live like you and Big Daddy.'"

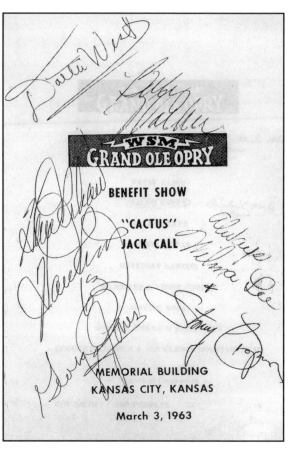

The program for the "Cactus" Jack Call benefit show, Patsy's last performance.

Patsy's final flight to Nashville departed from the Dyersburg airport.

Nashville Banner.

Nashville's Oldest Newspaper

LONG MAY OUR LAND BE BRIGHT WITH FREEDOM'S HOLY LIGHT; PROTECT US BY THY MIGHT, GREAT GOD, OUR KING

Founded April 10, 1876

VOL. LXXXVI. NO. 253 — NASHVILLE, TENN., WED. AFTERNOON, MAR. 6, 1963 — 46 PAGES — PRICE: TEN CENTS

4 OPRY STARS DIE IN CRASH

Plane Debris Yields Bodies At Camden

By LARRY BRINTON and CLAY HARGIS

Camden—The remains of four country music personalities, including three nationally-known Grand Ole Opry stars, were found this morning in the scattered bits of a private plane which crashed near here.

The victims were Patsy Cline, Cowboy Copas, Hawkshaw Hawkins and Randy Hughes, believed pilot of the ill-fated aircraft.

The wreckage was discovered about 6 a.m. after a night-long search by highway patrol, Civil Defense and local officers.

POLICE OFFICERS and funeral home attendants comb wreckage of a plane which crashed near Camden for parts of the bodies of four Grand Ole Opry personalities. The wreckage was strewn over an area of about 60 yards. Pieces of the single-engine plane hung in trees, along with some clothing.

★ ★ ★
Three Were Headliners
Opry Hit Hardest By Fatal Air Crash

By RED O'DONNELL
Television and Radio Editor

No Space On Plane
'God On My Side,' Says Billy Walker

Cuba Caves Said Hideout For Soviets

By FRANK VAN DER LINDEN
Banner's Washington Bureau

Senate Delays On Truck Weights Bill

By NEIL CUNNINGHAM
Chief of The Banner

'Round The Clock
WITH RED O'DONNELL
TALES OF ONE CITY

Woman Burned On Burial Pyre
In Ancient Rite

Weather Report

Temperatures

Cold Front May Mean Snow On Way

Don't Dare Miss Comics Showing

DO YOU HEAR ME?

CHARLIE BROWN invites that everyone visit the newspaper comics showing March 10 at the Parthenon. Details are on Page 12.

NEWS ROUNDUP

FEATURE INDEX — Page 12

PATSY CLINE

HAWKSHAW HAWKINS

COWBOY COPAS

RANDY HUGHES

THE NASHVILLE TENNESSEAN

Served by America's Greatest News Services

At the Crossroads of Natural Gas and TVA Power—Telephone Alpine 5-1221

VOL. 57—No. 309   Second Class Postage Paid at Nashville, Tenn.   NASHVILLE, TENN., THURSDAY MORNING, MARCH 7, 1963   ★ ★   10 CENTS   56 PAGES

FRANCE WARNS STRIKERS

Stars Warned Winds Dangerous

Dyersburg Airport Head Says Hughes Ignored Plea; Plane Crashed Hour Later

By GERALD HENRY, Staff Correspondent

CAMDEN, Tenn.—The crash of a light plane which killed four Grand Ole Opry personalities—three of whom were stars—came about 100 miles after the talent scout pilot was urged to stay overnight in Dyersburg.

Dyersburg Airport Manager Bill Braese said he tried to get Randy Hughes, 35, to forget about the night hop—but...

At 6:07 p.m. the pilot, Cowboy Copas, 49, Patsy Cline, 30, and Hawkshaw Hawkins, 41, roared down the runway and disappeared toward Nashville.

Irony Tinges Opry Deaths

By JULIE HOLLABAUGH

Today, scarcely 24 hours after a splintering plane crash took the lives of three of the most famous Grand Ole Opry stars, the last record cut by one of them will be in the mails.

Title of the record, by Cowboy Copas is "Goodbye Kisses." Included in the record is a significant edged in black expressing heartfelt sorrow of all his fans at the tragic death of the well-known country music entertainer.

"The record was cut in a session two weeks ago and we had planned the mailing," said Don Pierce, president of Starday Records. "We're going ahead with the mailing. We feel Copas would have wanted it that way."

The story of the tragic scene...

Aloft an hour later, in a quick, swirl before 24 miles settled down, the four died in tearing, twisting, diabolic plane crash.

"I TRIED TO get him to stay over because of the high winds on the way," Braese said.

Said Hughes said he was the fellow with the crew; he, the Nashville flight. He said he had already come from Kansas City and he was going ahead."

Mrs. Kathy Hughes of Nashville suffered a double tragedy in the mishap. Her husband was Randy Hughes, her father was Cowboy Copas.

The four were returning from Kansas City, where they had given a benefit performance for the family of Cactus Jack Call, a radio disc jockey killed in a traffic accident.

Riders Clutter

Liquor Law Showdown Set

Patsy Cline's soft gold slipper, covered with mud, points toward site where four-passenger plane crashed, digging out a deep hole that filled with water from an apparent rainfall.   —Staff photo by Gerald Holly

Regime Hints Of Rationing Coal and Gas

May Single Out Leaders of 200,000 Miners for Jailing

PARIS (AP) — The French government threatened new tough measures last night to end the six-day strike of 200,000 coal miners.

The imposition of coal and gas rationing loomed.

The announcement came after a meeting of President Charles de Gaulle and his cabinet. It brought a reaction of bitterness from union leaders in Northern France, where half the coal is mined. They said they are preparing for a long strike.

The government did not specify the action it would take.

A GOVERNMENT spokesman said the measures will coincide with a radio-television speech in two or three days by Premier Georges Pompidou. He added that if the situation worsened, de Gaulle himself may speak.

The government has not yet tried to enforce orders for the miners to return to the pits.

Informed sources speculated action may be taken against all the miners, but warned that key personnel and leaders could be singled out for prosecution in courts. They could be fined and jailed.

Pompidou declared earlier in the day that the miners would have to be back to work before they demands for more pay and a shorter work week will be discussed.

The day following Patsy's fatal crash, the local newspapers photographed her "soft gold slipper" at the site as well as Roger Miller looking over Hawkshaw Hawkins' boots.

seven

Patsy posing during the photo shoot for her last album, February 1963.

Sweet Dreams

Sweet dreams of you,
Ev'ry night I go through.
Why can't I forget you,
And start my life anew,
Instead of having sweet dreams about you?
You don't love me,
It's plain;
I should you know
You'll never wear my name.
I should hate you
The whole night through
Instead of having sweet dreams of you.

(Lyrics by Don Gibson, copyright 1955, 1983 by Acuff-Rose Music, Inc.)

"I t all came back to me, so clear," Joyce Blair recalls that last conversation with Patsy asking her to take care of her children should she die. "I thought, why did Patsy tell me this. She asked us to go to her children. That's exactly what we did. We locked our house up, took our little boy, and went straight to her home.

"Charlie said, 'Big Daddy, I've always had Randy to help, I'm asking for you and Blair to help me.' We tried to comfort Charlie as much as we could and stayed until her body left for Virginia to be buried. We tried to do what she asked and I hope we have fulfilled that part. We love the children so much."

JOYCE BLAIR

Charlie arranged to have Patsy's casket moved from the funeral home to her dream home to get her away from the curiosity seekers in Nashville. Her body was moved to Winchester for the funeral. Not surprisingly, Patsy's funeral was the largest Winchester has ever had, before or since. The flower shops ran out of flowers, as Charlie recalls. "Hubert Long arranged the whole funeral. He took me to pick out the casket and the flowers. The National Life Insurance Company, which owned WSM, sent this huge white cross for the top of the casket. They had a prayer service for Patsy, in Nashville. Randy had a cold.

"After the prayer service, her mother, and I guess her sister, took the kids and went back to Virginia. I went to the funeral home and God there was people. You could hardly get in. That was great, but there was also a bunch of curiosity seekers. I just seen all these people so I asked them to take Patsy's casket to the house (Patsy's dream house on Nella Drive).

CHARLIE DICK

"They did that a lot in Virginia. The people just meet at the home, instead of going to the funeral home. It just seemed the thing to do. Plus, we just got the new home and Patsy was so tickled with it. After I took her to the house, I had people coming from everywhere. I can remember looking in the kitchen. There was June Carter, Del Wood, and Felice Bryant, in my kitchen, washing dishes. I couldn't believe it, all these people we had looked upon as stars and here there are — just jumped right in and took care of everything.

"I stayed over another day to go to the Jack Anglin prayer

service. (Country singer Jack Anglin was killed in an automobile accident on his way to Patsy's prayer service.) Hubert arranged to have Patsy's body taken to Virginia. He packed up the white cross in a plastic bag and sprinkled it with water. In Virginia it looked like it was brand new. Hubert Long took care of all that, very nice man.

"It about whipped me. I remember going back to Winchester with Patsy's brother Sam and Billy Graves. There are very few people I ride with and sleep, but I slept half way home on that trip. I was just whipped. When I got there Randy was lying on the couch, just burning up with fever. I picked him up and rushed him straight to the doctor. The doctor sent him straight to the hospital. He stayed in the hospital with pneumonia. He was there when we had the funeral.

"Julie and I went to the funeral, along with Patsy's mother Hilda and everybody else. I can't tell you how many people were there. Floral shops were running out of flowers. The cemetery is probably four or five miles out of town and I think there were cars from the cemetery to the town."

As the local Winchester *Star* reported, "the highways were jammed for hours. . . . But apparently the drivers and their passengers didn't mind too much — they had seen what they wanted. Patsy got a funeral worthy of royalty."

Looking back on her life and career, Charlie Dick presents this eulogy for Patsy. "One of her biggest goals was to get to be a regular on the Grand Ole Opry — she sure done that. She would tear the Opry house down, which I think thrilled her very much. Of course, she wanted hit records, I am sure everybody did. Other than making life better for all of us, I think the Opry was probably the biggest goal she had. She wouldn't have given up the music — or the kids. We only had six-and-a-half years, but they were great years. I just wish they had never ended."

Patsy's daughter Julie has been able to appreciate her mother's talents and gifts even more so years after her death. "When I went to high school being Patsy Cline's daughter was nothing special. Nobody knew me as being different from anybody else. When I went back to my high school reunion, fifteen years later, all these people that I went to school with were coming up to me and saying, 'I didn't know that was your mother. I didn't know that was you. I saw the movie and I had no idea that was you.' That was really something — that was nice."

Patsy Cline's grave is marked by a bronze plaque with the epitaph, "Death cannot kill what never dies." Since her death, close friends and country artists have never stopped singing her praises, paying tribute to her talent, her courage, her character.

"If you're going to have a tragic accident," Patsy's friend and collaborator Harlan Howard remarks, "it's probably kind of neat that at least you did it giving your music away. It was just a gentle, loving, way to go." Howard continues his tribute recognizing Patsy's unique place in country music history as a consummate artist. "There are people like Patsy, George Jones, Ray Charles, great singers, and when you get a hit with them you almost never get another record. They nail it so good, it's so admired by the singers, that even twenty-five years later they don't want to do it on an album. Musically, Patsy's life history is built around *Walkin' After Midnight*, *I Fall to Pieces*, and *Crazy*. We just haven't had a lot of people wanting to mess with *I Fall To Pieces*. She did such a great job I think it kind of scares others off.

"After Patsy was killed I kept thinking — who's going to take Patsy's place? There are so many beautiful singers who have come along that I've loved — Connie Smith, Emmylou, Wynonna — just really great singers. But it just recently occurred to me that nobody ever replaces certain people that rise to stardom. You don't replace Lefty Frizzell or Ernest Tubb. She's just in that upper echelon, her and Jim Reeves, along with Ernest Tubb and a handful of people who caused other people to maybe emulate them and have and had an influence on them.

"You don't replace Patsy Cline. I've stopped looking for another Patsy Cline because there's not going to be one."

In Harold Bradley's opinion, "Patsy took the torch from Kitty Wells and she raised the level of the singers up to a standard. Now she is the standard. I just came back from Branson and I can't tell you how many people I heard singing *I Fall To Pieces*, *Sweet Dreams*, and *Crazy*. The beautiful part about Patsy's singing is that nobody can do it like she did it. You listen to those records and

JULIE FUDGE

HARLAN HOWARD

HAROLD BRADLEY

you get to the end of *Faded Love* where she does that little sigh and you could tell it was really for real. She was very convincing — she was a great storyteller. I am really proud of the history that I had with her, and I treasure the fact that I worked with, probably, the greatest singer — I think that you would have to say, the greatest country singer of all time."

In his tribute to Patsy, Roy Clark isolates Patsy as the greatest talent of her generation and traces her influence on subsequent female country singers. "She had that incredible talent that only comes along once in our generation — once in a lifetime. I hear her influence in female and male artists because she sang with so much feeling. If you're going to do songs with messages, and songs with emotion, then you go to the people who had the most. She's not just a female influence. Anyone that plays country music, or the fringes of country music, has to be influenced by Patsy Cline. Some of the young ones may not even realize it because it's been handed down. If she was still with us today, what other great milestones would she have reached and what would she be doing today? Her talents grew into the confidence in herself when she could take an unknown song and make it into such a smash hit. She would still be doing it today."

Hank Cochran shares this sentiment of 'what-might-have-been' if Patsy had not died just as her singing style had evolved to its zenith. "You can hear it. You can hear the difference from *I Fall To Pieces* to *Crazy*. The smoothness and how she was really getting into it. Boy! It's really sad when I think now what she would of done with that voice. There ain't been anybody to match it yet."

Roy Drusky pays tribute to Patsy's contribution to the country music industry, raising the profile of the music and crossing country with pop. "In my years as a member of the Grand Ole Opry I have seen a lot of talent — a lot of good talent. Patsy had the charisma, she had the magnetism that very few have. You have a lot of great singers that don't have the magnetism. You have a lot of singers who have magnetism but don't have a great singing voice. She was different. She had both. That's proven out by the fact that her songs are still well received, as well as played — they

ROY
CLARK

HANK
COCHRAN

ROY
DRUSKY

are classics. She was a definite stylist and stylists tend to last. Patsy was, without a doubt, a credit to the industry.

"There was nothing put on about her. If she didn't like you, you knew it. If she liked you, you knew it. She had a lot of compassion. Patsy was unique. I have to think that country music, and music in general, is a little bit better because Patsy Cline was part of it."

As Phil Whitney at WINC in Winchester describes Patsy's empathy and ambition, "she'd get down and dance with the crowd . . . she was part of it, she was in it all the way . . . that's her life . . . that's the way she lived."

George Hamilton IV has especially fond memories and an equally high regard for her talent as a performer and her character as a woman. "Patsy learned her craft — she perfected it. She became a polished entertainer and that stood her in good stead once she got to Nashville and then on to Las Vegas. I am sure if she had lived she would be one of the biggest stars today.

"I would like to underscore the point that you can talk about her personality, her charisma, the colorful sides to her personality, her earthiness and her saltiness. But, most importantly, the reason she's remembered today, in this music business, is because she was a great singer and a great stylist.

"When I moved to Nashville in late '59, Patsy was well established and had become a member of the Grand Ole Opry. She was cutting some great records. Her records weren't considered straight country. She was uptown. Her records were selling — pop and country. I can't think of another girl singer who was crossing over and having cross-over hits. Skeeter Davis did it with *The End Of The World*. It was a bit later. Patsy started hitting the pop charts before any of the girl singers. Her records stand up today. They sound like today's country records. Back then they were very progressive and very far ahead.

"She was a pioneer. She used orchestra, vocal groups, and strings. She was an uptown, country singer, but she never lost her country roots. She didn't pretend to be something she wasn't. She had a gift from God and she used it with authority — with confidence and taste. She was an artist."

Don Helms also recognizes how fresh, current, and relevant

Patsy Cline's music is today. "I think the lyrics on the songs Patsy did are very current. They are not dated to a certain period in time. She just took the songs into a different area. A lot of people would say, 'I'm not really a big country fan but I'm a big Patsy Cline fan.' I don't believe she realized how big she was. She was bigger than she thought she was."

As George Jones adds, "Patsy had the talent — she had the voice. Oh my goodness! All she had to do was just sing anybody's song and their record would quit selling and hers would start selling. She had that type of voice."

Jan Howard shares this sentiment about her dear friend. "I think it's phenomenal — you play her records today and they are timeless, they're current. Maybe it's part of God's plan, I don't know, because her voice was timeless. The recordings don't sound like the recordings of that time. I play my recordings from that time and they sound totally different. We had the same producer (Owen Bradley). I just think it was a plan because she wasn't going to be here all that long to give it in person so her music would live on forever — and it will."

Neil Matthews Jr. of The Jordanaires challenges anyone to compare Patsy's recordings with those of today's contemporary singers. "To really realize what a great singer Patsy Cline was take her record of say Crazy and play it. Then play Linda Ronstadt's record of Crazy. Play Patsy Cline's record of She's Got You and then play Loretta Lynn's record of She's Got You and many other stars who have recorded Patsy Cline's songs. If you compare them, you will soon realize what a great singer Patsy Cline really was."

Ferlin Husky pays tribute to Patsy for opening the doors for other country women in the business. "Patsy was a forerunner. A lot of people liked her singing, like Loretta Lynn, but Patsy was first. She was one of the first ones to hit really big before Tammy Wynette. There were other girls, in the past, that sang country songs but not like Patsy. They never got as popular. She was accepted, world-wide, with whatever type of music. She paved the way. She broke ground for the new girls. It's been easier for a lot of the country girl singers since Patsy. The door was opened. There was somebody in the country field who had broken into the pop field and went to Vegas."

Mavis Husky credits Patsy for "de-nasaling" country girl singers and making it possible for them to sing other kinds of music. "Patsy opened many doors for 'un-nasal' country girl singers. She really did. That was all there was to learn and it was boring because it all sounded the same. It was like a blossom. She opened that door for us to be able to sing other songs beside three-twangy, chord things. I still do all her songs. I never did see her do *Bill Bailey, Won't You Please Come Home* but that's one of my songs that I do all the time."

For Loretta Lynn, Patsy was not only a good friend but also her role model. "I think Patsy was probably the first woman to say what she felt. She was the first to record a song that went over to pop. She was the first one to be different — she was different on everything she had done. One of the things she taught me was how to do a song when I went on stage. She taught me how to go on stage and have it come off. She told me one day, now this is what the public expects but this is what I do. She meant that she wanted to please them but if it didn't please her, she wouldn't do it. I thought that was great to say. I've never been that strong — Patsy was a strong person. She was the first one in Nashville to step out of the boundaries and go with every direction when it came to music. Patsy was twenty-five years ahead of her time. I never heard anybody that has come as close to singing as great as Patsy. Patsy opened the doors for all the girls. She was great!"

Dale Turner agrees with Loretta. "Patsy was perfect on every song. You could just sit and listen to her all day and night. You didn't want to do anything else. You didn't want to dance you just wanted to sit and listen to her sing. She was the one who was pivotal because she did cross-over. She opened the doors period — for everyone in country music."

But Patsy was more than a forerunner. In a highly competitive business it is refreshing to hear so many contemporaries, such as Del Wood, single out Patsy, not only for her unquestioned singing ability but for her humanity. "She was so good to people. She helped Loretta Lynn — numerous people in the business. She left a shining example for everybody to try to emulate."

MAVIS HUSKY

LORETTA LYNN

DALE TURNER

DEL WOOD

143

Patsy's contemporaries are not the only generation of country artists to pay tribute to her talent and praise her character. Ronna Reeves was born three years after Patsy was killed and she is typical of the new country singers who discover Patsy Cline and become fans. "I discovered Patsy Cline through my mom's record collection. I started going through them and thought, Hey! This is different. This doesn't sound like some of the other women that are singing this country and western stuff. I thought she had one of the most beautiful voices and one the best ranges that I had heard from the very low notes up to the very high notes. I just thought she was great and I thought, well you know mom, you really did have some cool people to listen to when you were growing up. Patsy's singing definitely influenced my singing."

Lisa Stewart is another of the younger singers who was born after Patsy died. She acknowledges the legacy Patsy left and how she has influenced her singing. "The one thing that I really admire about her is the rich color in her voice. It's a little bit of a dark voice but that's something you're born with, or not. Another thing that I really love about her voice is her impeccable phrasing. She lays back on her phrasing and she just makes listeners kind of sit on the edge of their seats waiting for the next line."

Sylvia readily admits that she tries to emulate Patsy's emotional approach to a song. "When I heard Patsy, it was the first time I really started focusing in on what I wanted to accomplish with my music. It was the emotion that she could get across. I've heard a lot of people sing on record but I never heard anyone sing with such emotion. I just felt I could reach in and touch her. She had a voice that you could visualize. I've heard Owen Bradley say something about her voice being multi-textured. It had a presence of its own. I can't explain it. It's a strong enough thing that I feel like I know her without having met her."

Marsha Thornton carries the same high opinion of Patsy's achievement. "I think Patsy had an influence on a lot of women in country music through the years. I know she had a great influence on me. I've talked to some of the other women in country music, some my age, some a little older, some of the newcomers who said that basically they had about the same story as I do. They heard

Patsy's voice, they were already into music and she influenced them tremendously. I've heard Patty Loveless talk about Patsy being a great influence on her life as well."

Michelle Wright grew up listening to the music of Patsy Cline. "When I think about Patsy Cline, and the influence that she had on my life, I think she influences me more today than she did when I was growing up and listening to her music. I think of a woman who is very strong and that voice. That's what we all say — that voice. She was just so remarkable."

MICHELLE WRIGHT

When k.d. lang started to become interested in country music, she searched for a role model. She found Patsy Cline. "I started to get interested in country music and I was searching for someone to make sense for me. I was given a couple of Patsy Cline records for my twenty-first birthday. I listened to her sing and how Patsy and Owen Bradley incorporated blues, swing and some of the rockabilly stuff. Her sensibility was so pure and yet she incorporated all these types of music. She had a type of soul that is hard to find in a singer. Soul only comes from integrity. That applied experience, whether it's from this life or from a past life, or whatever, she had it. She felt pain, she felt joy, she was very passionate and I think that's very important in being a great singer. I loved her rockabilly a great deal, as much as I loved the ballads. I loved everything. I loved her sense of humor. I think she had a great sense of humor. She sang songs with a lot of dimension. She delivered with a lot of different attitudes at one time, which is important to me as well."

k.d. lang

Patsy Cline was probably the first female country singer Trisha Yearwood heard at the tender age of six. "There was one record that my parents had which was a compilation of country hits. They had everybody on there — like Hank Williams, Ernest Tubb, Roy Acuff and all those great traditional singers — and only two women on the record. One was Kitty Wells and one was Patsy Cline — it was I Fall To Pieces. I really clung to the women on that album because it was all that I had at the time and I was listening to country.

TRISHA YEARWOOD

"I'm a real admirer of singers who have real power and emotion in their singing. There are only two women I would name who do that — one is Linda Ronstadt, who is more contemporary, and Patsy. There is just this emotion where you believe every word. On some of the songs you hear the catch in her voice, you hear breath, and you feel like she's in the room with you, singing. There are not very many artists who can leave that kind of impression and make you really feel something. Patsy's definitely one of the few. She did whatever she wanted to and it comes through in her music. She definitely broke some rules. Somebody had to do it, and she was the one."

Perhaps the last word can be given to Dottie West, who spoke to her last the day before Patsy died and who herself died an untimely death in an automobile crash in 1991. "Patsy Cline was my idol, immediately, from the first time I heard her sing. Patsy could sing any kind of song and she just sang with so much emotion. She could put more emotion into it than the writer did. Her music is timeless. I think we'll always hear her music. It's still heard everyday on radio. She really said things with her music. She said things for people. There was feeling there.

"Patsy once said, 'Hoss! if you can't do it with feeling, don't.'"

The United States Postal Service commemorated Patsy with a special issue stamp in 1993.

Patsy's friends and fans have erected a bell tower (left) in her honor near Shenandoah Memorial park, where she rests. The inscription on her memorial reads "Death cannot kill what never dies." Another monument near Camden, Tennessee marks the site of the fatal plane crash (bottom).

Cline's husband anxious to set the record straight

BY JOHN HASLETT CUFF
The Globe and Mail

Patsy Cline: documentary features some great footage.

WHEN THE folks at Halfway Productions Inc. in Toronto decided to do a documentary on country singer **Patsy Cline**, they found a willing ally in her husband, **Charlie Dick**. According to **Doug Hall** (who is the father of producer Mark and director Greg Hall, who made The Real Patsy Cline), Dick was anxious to set the record straight. "Charlie wasn't too happy with the movie (**Sweet Dreams**, starring **Jessica Lange** and **Ed Harris**). He felt the real story should be told. He wanted to come out better than the wife-beating old lecher that Harris portayed him as," said Hall.

The results will be shown on First Choice on Dec. 2. It's a well-made, entertaining piece of work with some great footage of Cline performing. **Charlie Dick, Loretta Lynn, Carl Perkins, Dottie West** and **Willie Nelson** all appear, talking about their links to Cline, who many feel set the standard for all aspiring country crooners, before her death in a plane crash in 1963.

Charlie Dick (top) has defended the reputation and kept the memory of the real Patsy Cline alive.

COUNTRY MUSIC
HALL OF FAME
ELECTED 1973

PATSY CLINE

SEPTEMBER 8, 1932   MARCH 5, 1963
BORN VIRGINIA PATTERSON HENSLEY IN VIRGINIA, PATSY WILL
LIVE IN COUNTRY MUSIC ANNALS AS ONE OF ITS OUTSTANDING
VOCALISTS. TRAGICALLY, HER CAREER WAS CUT SHORT IN ITS
PRIME WHEN SHE WAS KILLED IN A PLANE CRASH. HER HERITAGE
OF RECORDINGS IS TESTIMONY TO HER ARTISTIC CAPACITY...
BIGGEST HIT, "I FALL TO PIECES," HAS BECOME A STANDARD.
CATAPULTED TO FAME BY AN ARTHUR GODFREY TALENT SCOUTS
APPEARANCE IN 1957. JOINED GRAND OLE OPRY 1960...
REALIZATION OF A LIFELONG AMBITION.
COUNTRY MUSIC ASSOCIATION

"I don't want to get rich . . . just live good." — Patsy Cline

SINGLES

JUNE 1, 1955

Hidin' Out
(EDDIE MILLER-
W.S.STEVENSON)

Turn The Cards Slowly
(SAMMY MASTERS)

A Church, A Courtroom Then Goodbye
(EDDIE MILLER-W.S. STEVENSON)

Honky Tonk Merry-Go-Round
(FRANK SIMON-STAN GARDNER)

January 5, 1956

Come On In (And Make Yourself At Home)
(V.F.STEWART)

I Cried All The Way To The Altar
(B. FLOURNOY)

I Don't Wanta
(EDDIE MILLER-W.F.STEVENSON-
DURWOOD HADDOCK)

I Love You Honey
(EDDIE MILLER)

April 22, 1956

Dear God
(V.F.STEWART)

Stop Look and Listen
(GEORGE LONDON-W.S.STEVENSON)

I've Loved And Lost Again
(EDDIE MILLER)
He Will Do For You
(What He's He's Done For Me)
(V.F. STEWART)

November 8, 1956

Walkin' After Midnight
(DON HECHT-ALAN BLOCK)

The Heart You May Break May Be Your Own
(TINY COLBERT)

Pick Me Up On Your Way Down
(BOB GEESLING)

A Poor Man's Roses (Or A Rich Man's Gold)
(BOB HILLIARD-MILTON DELUGG)

April 24, 1957

Fingerprints
(W.S. STEVENSON)

Today, Tomorrow And Forever
(DON REID)

A Stranger In My Arms
(CHARLOTTE WHITE-VIRGINIA HENSELY-
MARY LU JEANS)

Don't Ever Leave Me Again
(LILLIAN CLARBORNE-VIRGINIA HENSLEY-
JAMES CRAWFORD)

April 25, 1957

Try Again
(BOB SUMMERS-JERRY LEFORS)

Then You'll Know
(BOBBY LILE)

Too Many Secrets
(BOBBIE LILE)

Three Cigarettes In An Ashtray
(EDDIE MILLER-W.S.MILLER)

May 23, 1957

In Care Of The Blues
(EDDIE MILLER-W.S. STEVENSON)

That Wonderful Someone
(GERTRUDE BURG)

Hungry For Love
(EDDIE MILLER-W.S. STEVENSON)

I Don't Wanta
(E. MILLER-W.S.STEVENNSON-
DURWOOD HADDOCK)

*Ain't No Wheels On This Ship
(We Can't Roll)*
(W.D. CHANDLER-W.S.STEVENSON)

I Can't Forget
(W.S. STEVENSON-CARL BELEW)

December 13, 1957

Stop The World (And Let Me Off)
(CARL BELEW-W.S. STEVENSON)

Walking Dream
(HAL WILLIS-GINGER WILLIS)

Cry Not For Me
(DON HECHT-JACK MOON)

*If I Could See The World
(Through The Eyes Of a Child)*
(SAMMY MASTERS-RICHARD POPE-
TEX SUTTERWHITE)

February 13, 1958

Just Out Of Reach
(V.F.STEWART)

I Can See An Angel
(K.ADELMAN)

*Come On In (And Make
Yourself At Home)*
(V.F. STEWART)

Let The Teardrops Fall
(C.C.BEAM-C.L.JILES-W.S.STEVENSON)

Never No More
(RITA ROSS-ALAN BLACK)

If I Could Only Stay Asleep
(ETHEL BASSEY-WAYLOND CHANDLER)

January 8, 1959

I'm Moving Along
(JOHNNY STARR)

I'm Blue Again
(C.C. BEAM-C.L.JILES-W.S.STEVENSON)

Love, Love, Love Me Honey Do
(C.C. BEAM-C.L.JILES-W.S.STEVENSON)

January 9, 1959

Yes I Understand
(C.C.BEAM-W.S.STEVENSON-C.L.JILES)

Gotta A Lot Of Rhythm In My Soul
(BARBARA VAUGHAN-W.S. STEVENSON)

July 3, 1959

Life's Railway To Heaven
(ARR. W.S. STEVENSON)

Just a Closer Walk With Thee
(ARR. W.S. STEVENSON)

January 27, 1960

Love Sick Blues
(IRVING MILLS-CLIFF FRIEND)

How Can I Face Tomorrow
(C.C. BEAM-C.L JILES-W.S.STEVENSON)

There He Goes
(EDDIE MILLER-DURWOOD HADDOCK-
W.S.STEVENSON)

Crazy Dreams
(C.C.BEAM-C.L.JILES-W.S.STEVENSON)

November 16, 1960

I Fall To Pieces
(HANK COCHRAN-HARLAN HOWARD)

Shoes
(HANK COCHRAN-VELMA SMITH)

Lovin' In Vain
(FREDDIE HART)

August 17, 1961

True Love
(COLE PORTER)

San Antonio Rose
(BOB WILLS)

The Wayward Wind
(STAN LEBOWSKY-HERB NEWMAN)

A Poor Man's Rose (Or A Rich Man's Gold)
(BOB HILLAIARD-MILTON DELUGG)

August 21, 1961

Crazy
(WILLIE NELSON)

August 24, 1961

Who Can I Count On
(SAMMY MASTERS)

Seven Lonely Days
(EARL SHUMAN-ALDEN SHUMAN-
MARSHALL BROWN)

I Love You So Much It Hurts
(FLOYD TILLMAN)

Foolin' Around
(HARLAN HOWARD-BUCK OWENS)

I Love You Ever Been Lonely
(Have You Ever Been Blue)
(PETER DEROSE-GEORGE BROWN)

August 25, 1961

South Of The Border (Down Mexico Way)
(MICHAEL CARR-JIMMY KENNEDY)

Walkin' After Midnight
(DON HECHT-ALAN BLOCK)

Strange
(MEL TILLIS-FRED BURCH)

You're Stronger Than Me
(HANK COCHRAN-JIMMY KEY)

December 17, 1961

She's Got You
(HANK COCHRAN)

February 12, 1962

You Made Me Love You
(I Didn't Want To Do It)
(JOE MCCARTHY-JAMES V. MONACO)

You Belong To Me
(PEE WEE KING-REDD STEWART-
CHILTON PRICE)

Heartaches
(AL HOFFMAN-JOHN KLENNER)

Your Cheatin' Heart
(HANK WILLIAMS)

February 13, 1962

That's My Desire
(HELMY KRESA-CARROLL LOVEDAY)

Half As Much
(CURLEY WILLIAMS)

February 15, 1962

Lonely Street
(CARL BELEW-W.S. STEVENSON-
KENNY SOWDER)

Anytime
(HERBERT HAPPY LAWSON)

*You Were Only Fooling
(While I was Falling In Love)*
(LARRY FOTINE-BILLY FABER-
FRED MEADOWS)

*I Can't Help It (If I Am Falling
In Love With You)*
(HANK WILLIAMS)

February 28, 1962

You're Stronger Than Me
(HANK COCHRANE-JIMMY KEY)

*When I Get Through With You
(You'll Love Me Too)*
(HARLAN HOWARD)

Imagine That
(JUSTIN TUBB)

So Wrong
(CARL PERKINS-DONNY DILL-MEL TILLIS)

September 5, 1962

Why Can't He Be You
(HANK COCHRAN)

Your Kinda Love
(ROY DRUSKY)

When You Need A Laugh
(HANK COCHRAN)

Leavin' On Your Mind
(WAYNE WALKER-WEBB PIERCE)

September 10, 1962

Back In Baby's Arms
(BOB MONTGOMERY)

Tra Le La Le La Triangle
(MARIJOHN WILKIN-FRED BURCH)

That's How A Heartache Begins
(HARLAN HOWARD)

February 4, 1963

Faded Love
(JOHN WILLS-BOB WILLS)

Someday (You'll Want Me To Want You)
(JIMMIE HODGES)

Love Letters In The Sand
(J.FRED COOTS-NICK KENNY-
CHARLES KENNY)

February 5, 1963

Blue Moon Of Kentucky
(BILL MONROE)

Sweet Dreams (Of You)
(DON GIBSON)

Always
(IRVING BERLIN)

February 6, 1963

Does Your Heart Beat For Me
(RUSS MORGAN-ARNOLD JOHNSON-
MITCHEL PARRISH)

Bill Bailey Won't You Please Come Home
(HUGHIE CANNON)

February 7, 1963

He Called Me Baby
(HARLAN HOWARD)

Crazy Arms
(CHUCK SEALS-RALPH MOONEY)

You Took Him Off My Hands.
(HARLAN HOWARD-WYNN STEWART-
SKEETS MCDONALD)

I'll Sail My Ship Alone.
(HENRY BERNARD-HENRY THURSTON-
LOSIS MANN-MORRY BURNS)

ALBUMS

5 August 1957 **PATSY CLINE**

27 November 1961 **SHOWCASE**
(WITH THE JORDANAIRES)

6 August 1962 **SENTIMENTALLY YOURS**

16 June 1963 **THE PATSY CLINE STORY**

NOTES OF INTEREST:

Most Nashville recording sessions ran
from 12:00 to 6:00 pm; 1:00 to 5:45 pm;
or 7:00 to 11:45 pm.

On the 24 April 1957 session Patsy
recorded two songs she co-wrote under
her maiden name Virgina Hensley: *Stranger
In My Arms* and *Don't Ever Leave Me Again*.

Beginning with the 25 April 1957 session, and up to the 13 February 1958
session, the Anita Kerr singers sang
backup for Patsy. The Anita Kerr singers
comprised: Anita Kerr; Dottie Dillard;
Louis Nuley and Gil Wright.

On the 23 May 1957 recording session
the bass player was Owen Bradley who
went on to become Patsy's producer.
The 8 January 1959 was the first session
that The Jordanaires sang backup for
Patsy. They continued as backup, until
Patsy's final session on 7 February 1963.

The Jordanaires were Hoyt Hawkins; Neal Matthews Jr.; Gordon Stoker; and Ray Walker.

Patsy had many of the top Nashville session players backing her up.

Acoustic
Bass: Bob Moore
Joe Zinkan

Cello: Byron Bach

Acoustic
Guitar: Harold Bradley
Randy Hughes
Jack Shook

Drums: Farris Coursey
Murrey Buddy Harman
Doug Kirkham

6-String
Electric
Bass: Harold Bradley
Wayne Moss

Electric
Guitar: Harold Bradley
Hank Garland
Grady Martin

Fiddle: Tommy Jackson
Organ: Floyd Cramer
Bill Pursell

Piano: Owen Bradley
Floyd Cramer
Hargus Pig Robbins

Steel
Guitar: Walter Haynes
Don Helms
Ben Keith

Harmonica: Charlie McCoy

Violin: Brenton Banks
George Binkley III
Cecil Brower
Lillian Hunt
Howard Carpenter
Solie Fott
Martin Katahn
Suzanne Parker
Verne Richardson
Michael Semanitzky
Wilda Tinsley
Gary Williams

Viola: Cecil Brower
John Bright

Vocals: Anita Kerr Singers
The Jordanaires

The arrangers for the majority of Patsy's recordings were Bill McElhiney and Bill Justis.

Beginning with the 8 January 1958 session all songs were recorded in both mono and stereo.

PRINCIPAL SOURCE OF INFORMATION:

The Patsy Cline Collection (compiled by the Country Music Foundation)

Authorized video biographies
written, directed, and produced
by Hallway Entertainment,
distributed by Buena Vista
Home Entertainment (left)
and White Star (bottom).

This book could not have been written if it hadn't been for the skills of my two sons, Mark who directed and Gregory who produced the authorized video biographies, *The Real Patsy Cline* and *Remembering Patsy*. I thank Mark and Greg for their confidence in allowing me the privilege of writing this book and for their support. I also thank my daughter Diane for her skill in transcribing over 600 pages of taped interviews and her husband, my son-in-law, Gordon for assisting her. I want to thank Charlie Dick sincerely, a valued friend, for the privilege of allowing me to tell the story of his wife, the incomparable Patsy Cline. As with all my books, my wife, Joyce, provided her editing and proofreading skills. Without her, I'd be lost.

Doug Hall

Photo Credits

Patsy Cline Estate: cover, pp. 7, 13, 93, 135.

Country Music Foundation: pp. 2, 25, 37, 57, 74, 90, 108, 110 (top), 111, 113, 151.

Jimmy Walker: pp. 38 (top), 72 (top and middle), 110 (bottom).

Sue Wilden: p. 38 (bottom), 148 (left and top).

Kent Florence: p. 148 (bottom).

All other photos courtesy of Hallway Entertainment from the video biographies *The Real Patsy Cline* and *Remembering Patsy*.

QUARRY MUSIC BOOKS

❑ *Neil Young: Don't Be Denied*
by JOHN EINARSON $21.95 CDN / $15.95 USA

❑ *Magic Carpet Ride: John Kay & Steppenwolf*
by JOHN KAY and JOHN EINARSON $21.95 CDN / $15.95 USA

❑ *American Woman: The Guess Who*
by JOHN EINARSON $21.95 CDN / $15.95 USA

❑ *Building a Mystery: Sarah McLachlan*
by JOHN EINARSON $21.95 CDN / $15.95 USA

❑ *Encyclopedia of Canadian Rock, Pop & Folk Music*
by RICK JACKSON $26.95 CDN / $19.95 USA

❑ *Encyclopedia of Canadian Country Music*
by RICK JACKSON $26.95 CDN / $19.95 USA

❑ *Celtic Tides*
by MARTIN MELHUISH $21.95 CDN / $15.95 USA

❑ *Snowbird: Anne Murray*
by BARRY GRILLS $21.95 CDN / $15.95 USA

❑ *The Hawk: Ronnie Hawkins and The Hawks*
by IAN WALLIS $21.95 CDN / $15.95 USA

❑ *Ironic: Alanis Morissette*
by BARRY GRILLS $21.95 CDN / $15.95 USA

❑ *For What It's Worth: Buffalo Springfield*
by JOHN EINARSON $21.95 CDN / $15.95 USA

❑ *Falling Into You: Céline Dion*
by BARRY GRILLS $21.95 CDN / $15.95 USA

❑ *The Mamas and The Papas*
by DOUG HALL $21.95 CDN / $15.95 USA

Available at your favorite bookstore or directly from the publisher:
Quarry Press, P.O. Box 1061, Kingston, ON K7L 4Y5, Canada.
Tel. (613) 548-8429, Fax. (613) 548-1556, E-mail: order@quarrypress.com.

Name _____

Address _____

_____ Postal Code _____ Telephone _____

Visa/Mastercard# _____ Expiry _____

Signature _____   Your books will be shipped with an invoice
                                            enclosed, including shipping costs, payable
                                            within 30 days in Canadian or American currency
                                            (credit card, check, or money order).